# BLOND'S TORTS

**S&G** **SULZBURGER & GRAHAM PUBLISHING, Ltd.**
**NEW YORK**

(800) 366-7086

# Abbreviations used in this book

**S.Ct.** - United States Supreme Court

**Ke** - Keeton, Keeton, Sargentich & Steiner, Tort and Accident Law, Cases and Materials (Second Edition, 1989)

**Ep** - Epstein, Cases and Materials on Torts (Fifth Edition, 1990)

**Fr** - Franklin & Rabin, Tort Law and Alternatives (Fifth Edition, 1992)

# BLOND'S TORTS

## Third Edition

**by**
**Neil C. Blond**

Third Edition
revised and edited
by
**Robert Connors**
**Susan R. Friedman**

## ALSO AVAILABLE IN THIS SERIES:

*Blond's Administrative Law*
*Blond's Civil Procedure*
*Blond's Constitutional Law*
*Blond's Contracts*
*Blond's Corporate Tax*
*Blond's Corporations*
*Blond's Criminal Law*
*Blond's Criminal Procedure*
*Blond's Essay Questions — Contracts*
*Blond's Essay Questions — Torts*
*Blond's Evidence*
*Blond's Family Law*
*Blond's Income Tax*
*Blond's International Law*
*Blond's Multistate Questions*
*Blond's Professional Responsibility Questions*
*Blond's Property*
*Blond's Torts*

PRINTED OCTOBER 1993
© 1992 SULZBURGER & GRAHAM PUBLISHING, LTD.

ISBN 0-945819-24-2
PRINTED IN THE UNITED STATES OF AMERICA

## Text Correlation

| Blond's Torts | Keeton Keeton Sargentich Steiner | Epstein Gregory Kalven | Franklin Rabin |
|---|---|---|---|
| **Chapter 1** Introduction to Tort Law | 1-24 | | 1-23 |
| **Chapter 2** Intentional Wrongs and Privileges | 25-122 | 3-60 1003-1036 | 795-868 |
| **Chapter 3** Negligence | 123-235 | 61-276 | 24-115 |
| **Chapter 4** The Duty of Care | 236-279 | 461-534 | 116-257 |
| **Chapter 5** Basic Defenses | 280-330 | 277-362 841-880 | 381-441 |
| **Chapter 6** Causation of Harm | 331-370 | 363-407 | 282-334 |
| **Chapter 7** Proximate Cause | 371-422 | 408-460 1037-1064 | 335-380 |
| **Chapter 8** Compensation for Harm | 423-458 | 731-814 | 626-670 |
| **Chapter 9** The Impact of Insurance | 459-503 | 881-912 | 671-715 |
| **Chapter 10** Imputed Liability | 504-527 | 815-840 | |

| Blond's Torts | Keeton Keeton Sargentich Steiner | Epstein Gregory Kalven | Franklin Rabin |
|---|---|---|---|
| **Chapter 11** Strict Liability | 528-571 | 535-570 | 442-481 |
| **Chapter 12** Nuisance | 572-634 | 571-610 | 601-625 |
| **Chapter 13** Products Liability | 635-755 | 611-730 | 482-600 |
| **Chapter 14** Alternative Compensation Systems | 756-975 | 913-1002 | 716-794 |
| **Chapter 15** Misrepresentation | 976-1052 | 1263-1302 | 1137-1151 |
| **Chapter 16** Defamation | 1053-1246 | 1065-1196 | 869-1045 |
| **Chapter 17** Misuse of Legal Procedure | 1247-1275 | | |
| **Chapter 18** Privacy | 1276-1303 | 1197-1262 | 1046-1136 |
| **Chapter 19** Interference With Advantageous Relationships | 1304-1308 | 1303-1356 | 258-281 1152-1190 |

# TABLE OF CONTENTS

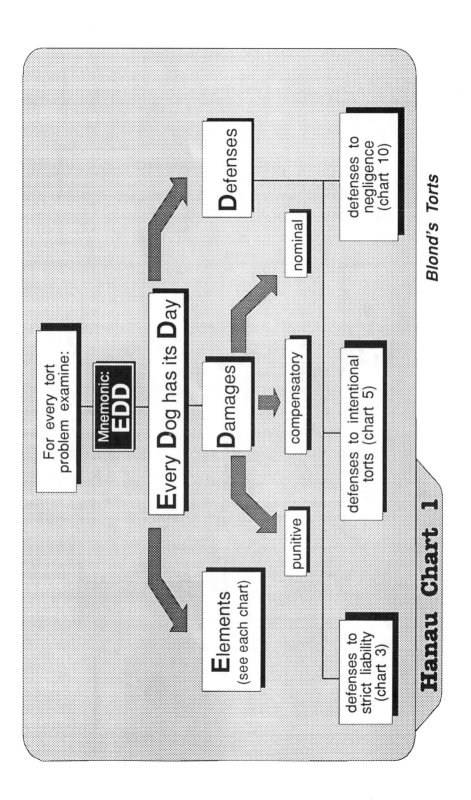

For every tort problem examine:

Mnemonic: **EDD**

**E**very **D**og has its **D**ay

**E**lements
(see each chart)

**D**amages

punitive

compensatory

nominal

**D**efenses

defenses to strict liability (chart 3)

defenses to intentional torts (chart 5)

defenses to negligence (chart 10)

*Blond's Torts*

**Hanau Chart 1**

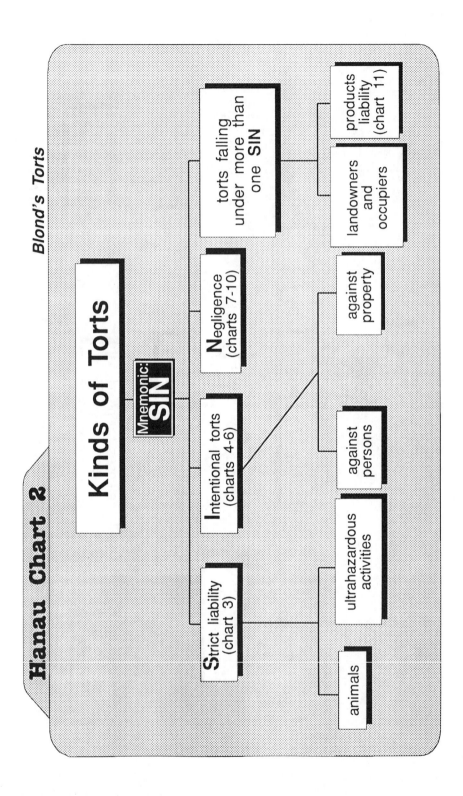

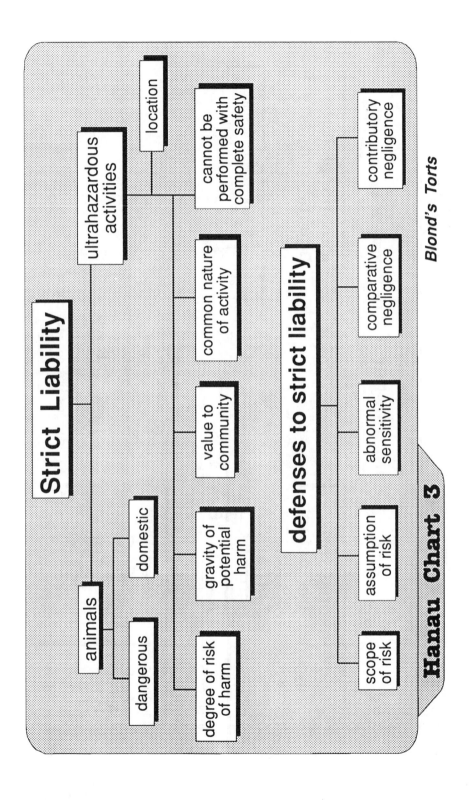

Blond's Torts

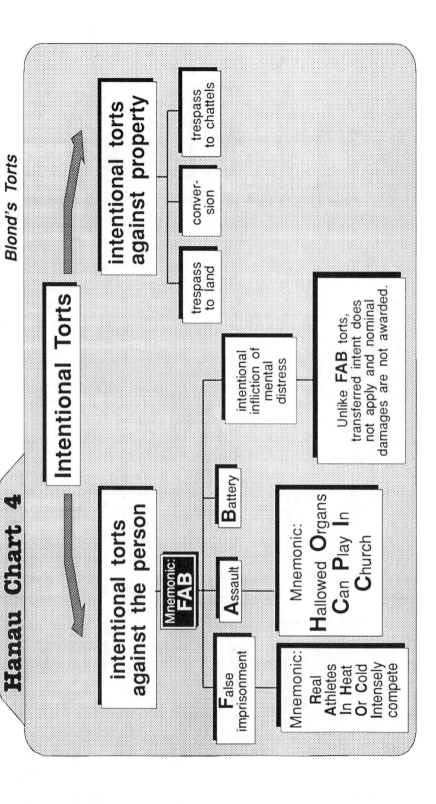

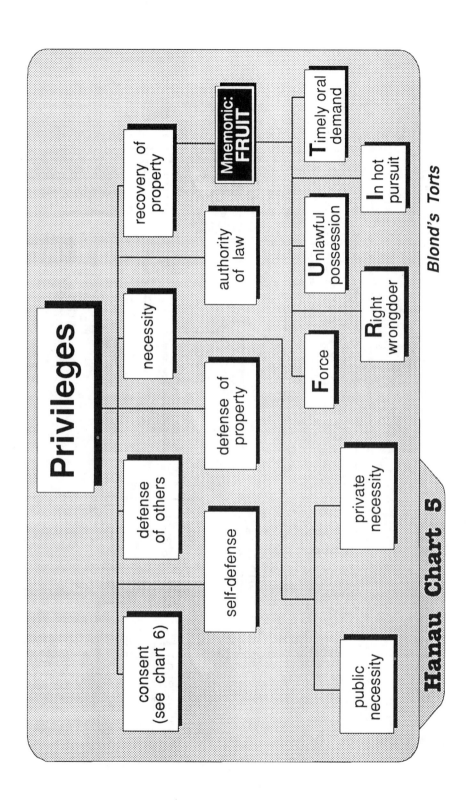

Privileges

- consent (see chart 6)
- defense of others
- self-defense
- necessity
  - defense of property
  - public necessity
  - private necessity
- authority of law
- recovery of property

Mnemonic: FRUIT

- **F**orce
- **R**ight wrongdoer
- **U**nlawful possession
- **I**n hot pursuit
- **T**imely oral demand

*Blond's Torts*

**Hanau Chart 5**

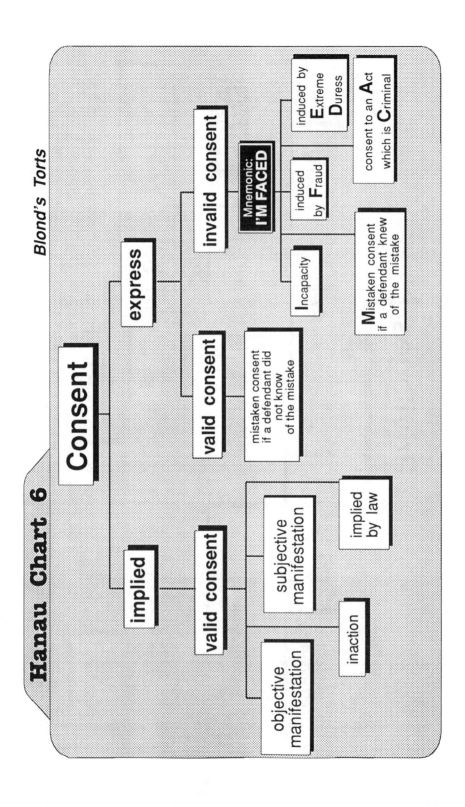

Hanau Chart 6

*Blond's Torts*

**Consent**

- implied
  - valid consent
    - objective manifestation
      - inaction
    - subjective manifestation
      - implied by law
- express
  - valid consent
    - mistaken consent if a defendant did not know of the mistake
  - invalid consent

    Mnemonic: **I'M FACED**
    - **I**ncapacity
      - **M**istaken consent if a defendant knew of the mistake
    - induced by **F**raud
    - induced by **E**xtreme **D**uress
      - consent to an **A**ct which is **C**riminal

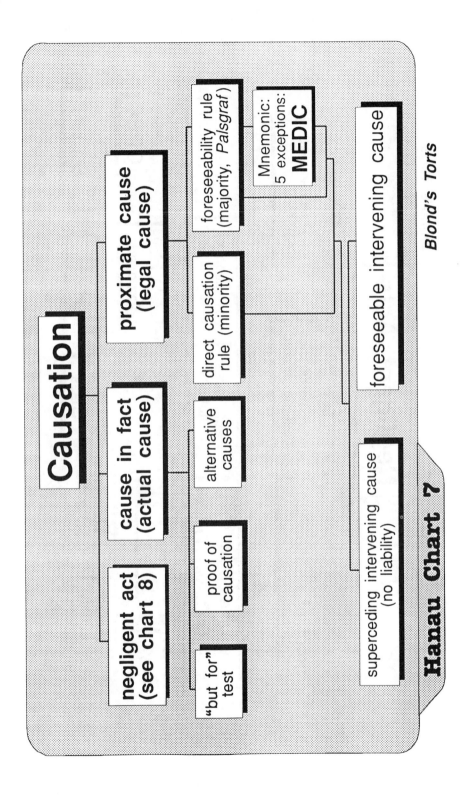

# Causation

**negligent act (see chart 8)**

**cause in fact (actual cause)**

**proximate cause (legal cause)**

"but for" test

proof of causation

alternative causes

direct causation rule (minority)

foreseeability rule (majority, *Palsgraf*)

Mnemonic: 5 exceptions: **MEDIC**

superceding intervening cause (no liability)

foreseeable intervening cause

# Hanau Chart 8

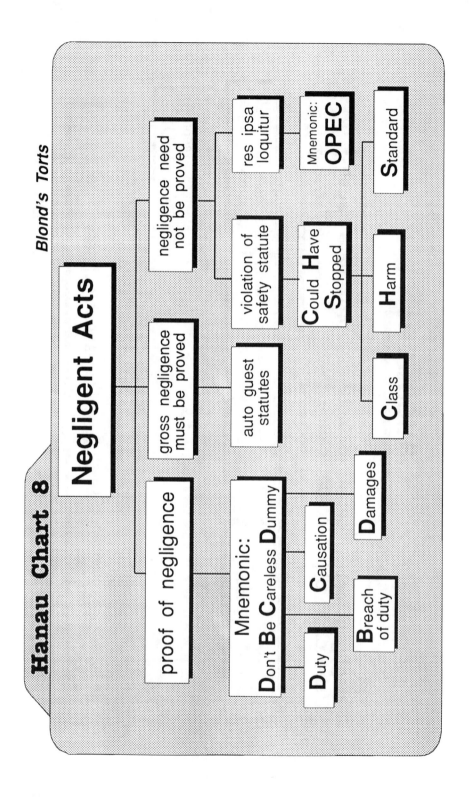

## Negligent Acts

- **proof of negligence**
  - Mnemonic: **D**on't **B**e **C**areless **D**ummy
    - **D**uty
    - **B**reach of duty
    - **C**ausation
    - **D**amages

- **gross negligence must be proved**
  - auto guest statutes

- **negligence need not be proved**
  - violation of safety statute
    - **C**ould **H**ave **S**topped
      - **C**lass
      - **H**arm
  - res ipsa loquitur
    - Mnemonic: **OPEC**
      - **S**tandard

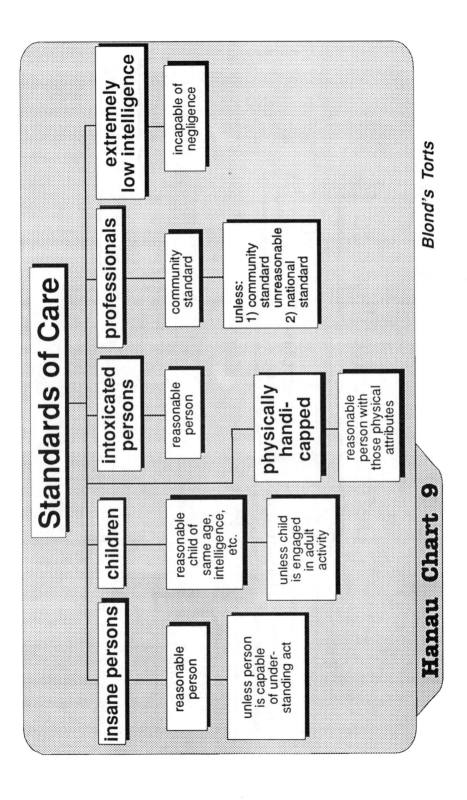

# Standards of Care

**insane persons**
- reasonable person
  - unless person is capable of understanding act

**children**
- reasonable child of same age, intelligence, etc.
  - unless child is engaged in adult activity

**intoxicated persons**
- reasonable person

**physically handicapped**
- reasonable person with those physical attributes

**professionals**
- community standard
  - unless:
    1) community standard unreasonable
    2) national standard

**extremely low intelligence**
- incapable of negligence

Hanau Chart 9

*Blond's Torts*

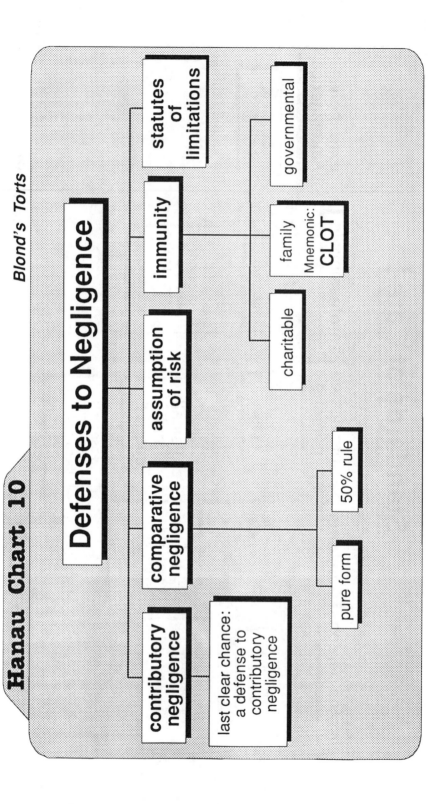

# Defenses to Negligence

- contributory negligence
  - last clear chance: a defense to contributory negligence
- comparative negligence
  - pure form
  - 50% rule
- assumption of risk
- immunity
  - charitable
  - family
  - Mnemonic: CLOT
  - governmental
- statutes of limitations

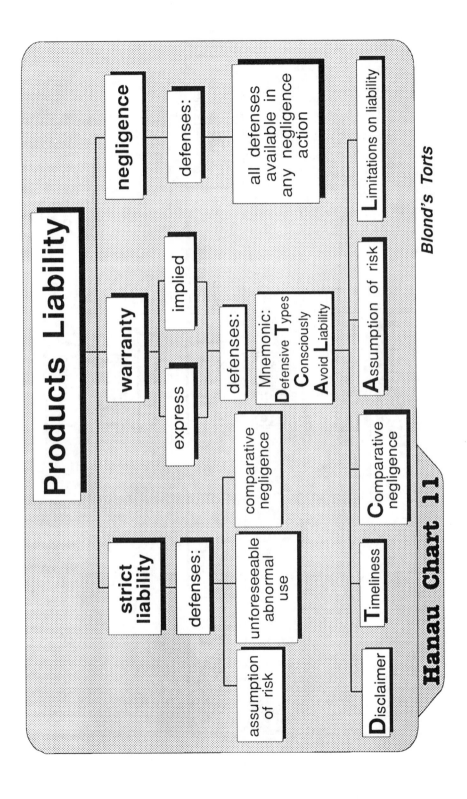

# Products Liability

**negligence**

- defenses:
  - all defenses available in any negligence action

**warranty**

- express
- implied
- defenses:
  - Mnemonic:
    **D**efensive **T**ypes **C**onsciously **A**void **L**iability
    - **D**isclaimer
    - **T**imeliness
    - **C**omparative negligence
    - **A**ssumption of risk
    - **L**imitations on liability

**strict liability**

- defenses:
  - assumption of risk
  - unforeseeable abnormal use
  - comparative negligence

*Blond's Torts*

**Hanau Chart 11**

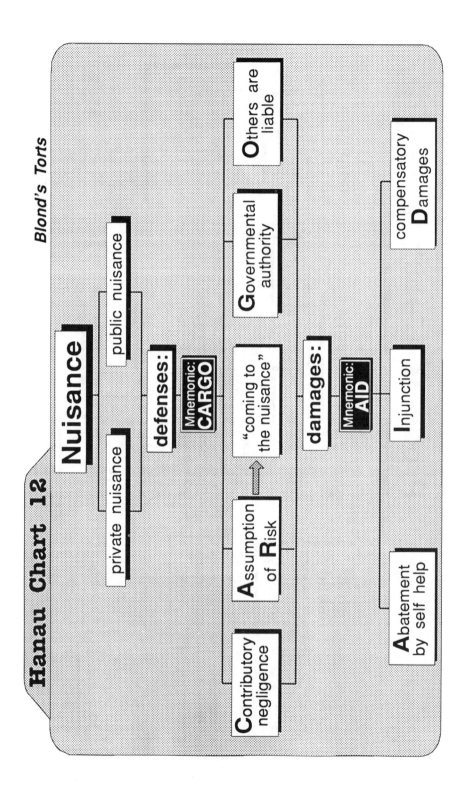

**Hanau Chart 12**

*Blond's Torts*

# Nuisance

- private nuisance
- public nuisance

**defenses:**
**Mnemonic: CARGO**

- **C**ontributory negligence
- **A**ssumption of **R**isk → "coming to the nuisance"
- **G**overnmental authority
- **O**thers are liable

**damages:**
**Mnemonic: AID**

- **A**batement by self help
- **I**njunction
- compensatory **D**amages

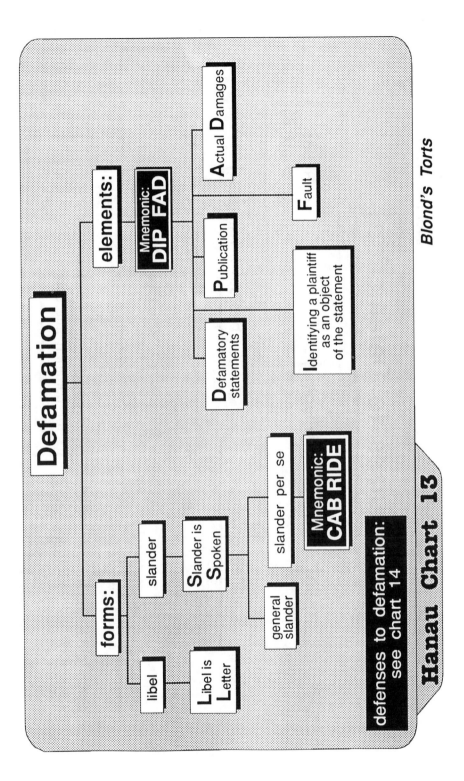

# Defamation

**forms:**

libel — Libel is Letter

slander — Slander is Spoken

slander per se — Mnemonic: **CAB RIDE**

general slander

**elements:**

Mnemonic: **DIP FAD**

Defamatory statements

Publication

Identifying a plaintiff as an object of the statement

Actual Damages

Fault

defenses to defamation: see chart 14

*Blond's Torts*

**Hanau Chart 13**

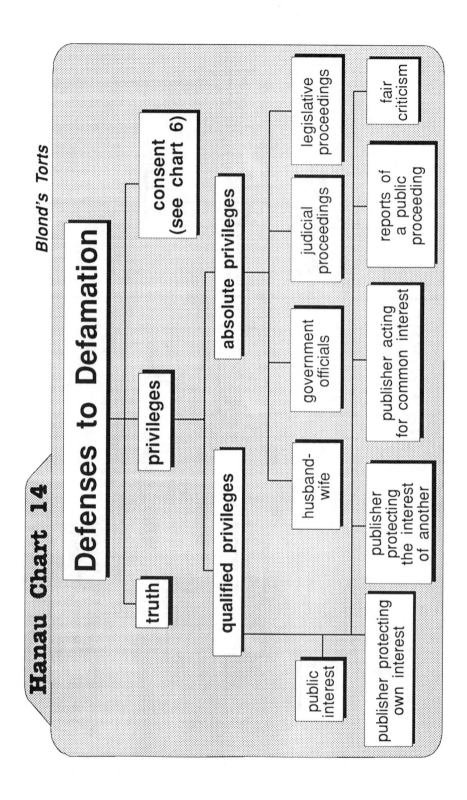

# Defenses to Defamation

- truth
- privileges
  - consent (see chart 6)
- qualified privileges
  - public interest
  - publisher protecting own interest
  - publisher protecting the interest of another
- absolute privileges
  - husband-wife
  - government officials
  - judicial proceedings
  - legislative proceedings
  - publisher acting for common interest
  - reports of a public proceeding
  - fair criticism

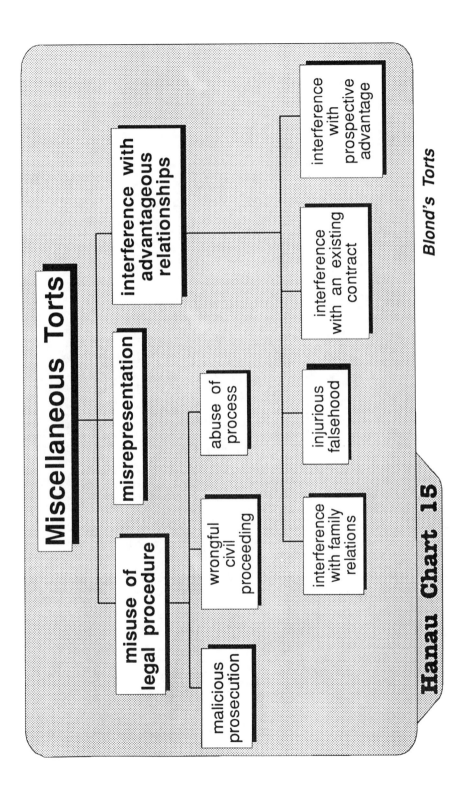

# Miscellaneous Torts

- misuse of legal procedure
  - malicious prosecution
  - wrongful civil proceeding
  - abuse of process
- misrepresentation
  - interference with family relations
  - injurious falsehood
- interference with advantageous relationships
  - interference with an existing contract
  - interference with prospective advantage

**Hanau Chart 15**

*Blond's Torts*

# Chapter 1

## INTRODUCTION TO TORT LAW

I.   DEFINITION

A tort is a private wrong, independent of a contract, resulting from a breach of duty.

II.  DEALING WITH TORT LAW

A.   First
When discussing any tort, always consider the following:

Mnemonic: **Every Dog has its Day**

1. Elements of torts present?

   a. Act

   b. Intent

   c. Causation

2. Are there any Defenses?

3. What are the possible Damages?

B.   Second
Next consider the conduct of one who has committed a tort:

Mnemonic: **SIN**

1. Strict Liability

2. Intentional

3. Negligent

## CASE CLIPS

### Garratt v. Dailey (1955) Ke, Fr

**Facts:** Dailey, age 5, pulled a chair from under Garratt knowing she was about to sit down.

**Issue:** May one be liable for battery without an intent to harm?

**Rule:** The "intent" element of battery is fulfilled if one knew with "substantial certainty" that contact would occur.

### Blyth v. Birmingham Waterworks Co. (1856) Ke, Ep

**Facts:** Blyth's house was damaged when a fire hydrant, installed by Birmingham, sprung a leak due to a severe and unusual frost. The hydrant had worked properly for 25 years prior to the incident.

**Issue:** Is it negligence to fail to plan for a rare and extraordinary situation?

**Rule:** Negligence involves the omission of an action that a reasonable person would perform, or acting in a way that a prudent and reasonable person would not.

### Kohlman v. Hyland (1926) Ke

**Facts:** The defendant's employee was involved in a car accident while on a detour from his business route, injuring Hyland. The employee had gone to visit his sister.

**Issue:** Is a detour for personal reasons during a business trip considered to be within the scope of employment for purposes of vicarious liability?

**Rule:** If an employee's physical deviation from a business route is reasonably foreseeable, an employer will be vicariously liable.

### Exner v. Sherman Power Construction Co. (1931) Ke

**Facts:** Exner was injured by an explosion of the defendant's dynamite. The defendant had taken all the necessary precautions in storing and using the dynamite.

**Issue:** Is a party liable for injuries resulting from an ultrahazardous activity even though the party exercised due care?

**Rule:** One is strictly liable, regardless of fault, for injuries caused by ultrahazardous activities.

### Whetro v. Awkerman (1970) Ke

**Facts:** Whetro was injured when a tornado destroyed his place of employment. His employers claimed no liability because the tornado was an "Act of God," as opposed to a work related hazard.

**Issue:** Are injuries resulting from "Acts of God" during the course of employment compensable under the Worker's Compensation Act?

**Rule:** It is no longer necessary to establish a relationship of proximate causality between employment and an injury to establish compensability under the Worker's Compensation Act. It is not a defense that the injury was caused by an "Act of God."

### Hammontree v. Jenner (1971) Fr

**Facts:** Jenner had a past history of epileptic seizures. After 14 years without a seizure, one occurred causing him to have a car accident in which Hammontree was injured. Jenner had a valid driver's license and the authorities knew of his condition.

**Issue:** Is there strict liability for accidents occurring due to sudden forces beyond a defendant's control?

**Rule:** An accident caused by a force outside one's control will not lead to liability. However, if the person knew or should have known that the uncontrollable force was likely to come on suddenly, the person's conduct may be negligent.

### Morrison v. National Broadcasting Co., Inc. (1965) Fr

**Facts:** The plaintiff participated in the defendant's rigged game show, believing it to be honest and authentic. When the truth was told, the plaintiff, a student, suffered harm to his reputation. While morally reprehensible, the defendant's actions were not illegal.

**Issue:** Is there a tort action for damages that are caused by a legal activity that violates moral expectations but does not fit under a recognized tort category?

**Rule:** The inability of a plaintiff to fit a tort action into one of the classical categories will not prevent recovery for an act that is corrupt by conventional standards or intentional as to its consequences.

# Chapter 2

## INTENTIONAL WRONGS AND PRIVILEGES

I.  **INTENT**

A.  Definition
Intent is generally defined as a purpose to bring about the invasion of another's protected interest by an act, or a failure to act when there is a legal duty to do so.

  1.  An Act
  An act is defined as a *voluntary* movement of the muscles.

  2.  The Invasion of Another's Protected Interest
  The desire to invade another's protected interest is not necessarily the same as the desire to harm, or the desire to bring about specific consequences.

  Example:
  Susan kicked Rob as a practical joke, honestly believing that Rob would not be harmed by the kick. Unfortunately, Rob's leg was particularly weak, and was fractured by the kick.
  Result: Susan has the necessary intent to be liable for Rob's injuries. Even though she did not desire to harm Rob, or to specifically cause the leg to fracture, she intended to kick, which was an intentional invasion of Rob's interest in being free from harmful or offensive contact, an interest which is protected by the tort of battery.

B.  Distinction between Specific Intent and General Intent

  1.  Difference

    a.  Specific Intent
    Tortfeasor's goal was to bring about consequences.

b. General Intent
Tortfeasor knew "with substantial certainty" that consequences would result.

2. Legal Significance
<u>Either</u> specific intent or general intent will satisfy the intent requirement for an intentional tort. If the "substantial certainty" test is not met, the tortfeasor may be liable for negligence, but not for an intentional tort.

C. Transferred Intent

1. Applicability
   a. Transferred intent is only applied to the torts of:

   Mnemonic: **FAB**

   i. **F**alse Imprisonment,

   ii. **A**ssault, and

   iii. **B**attery

   b. Transferred intent is only applied if the harm resulting from the tort is direct and immediate, as opposed to consequential.

2. Ways of Transfer

   a. If a party intends to commit a tort against one person but a second person is injured, the tortfeasor is held to have the intent necessary for liability to the second person.

   Example:
   Rob shot at Susan, but missed. The bullet hit Brett, a bystander.
   Result: Rob is liable for a battery to Brett, even though he only intended a battery upon Susan.

b. If an actor intends to commit one intentional tort but actually commits a different intentional tort, he is held to have the intent necessary for the second tort.

Example:
Rob intended to scare Susan by throwing a baseball in her direction. Susan did not see the ball because her back was turned, but the baseball struck Brett.
Result: Rob is liable for a battery to Brett, even though he only intended to assault Susan.

D.    Minors and Incompetents
The majority of jurisdictions hold that both minors and insane persons may have the competence to formulate the necessary intent to commit an intentional tort.

## II.    BATTERY

A.    Definition
Battery is defined as the causing of harmful or offensive contact to the plaintiff's person with the intent to make contact.

Mnemonic: **H**allowed **O**rgans **C**an **P**lay **I**n **C**hurch

1. **H**armful or **O**ffensive **C**ontact

   a. Harmful or offensive contact is determined by the reasonable person standard, i.e., whether a reasonable person would consider such contact harmful or offensive to one's dignity or honor.

   b. A plaintiff does not have to be aware of the contact. For example, a valid battery occurs when someone is spit upon while sleeping.

   c. Harmful or offensive contact may be either direct or indirect. For example, if Rob punches Susan, this is direct contact. If Rob throws a baseball at Susan, this is indirect contact.

2. Plaintiff's Person
A plaintiff's person includes not only the body, but also objects closely associated with the body, such as clothing, a cane, an object in hand, and dentures.

3. Intent to Make Contact
One does not need to intend harm to another — rather an intent to cause contact is sufficient. Also, remember that transferred intent applies to battery. See Ch. 2, I, C.

B. Damages
Actual damages are not necessary; a plaintiff may recover nominal damages. Punitive damages are available in cases of outrageous conduct. A plaintiff may recover for both mental and physical harm.

III. ASSAULT

A. Definition
Assault is defined as the intentional act of causing a reasonable apprehension of immediate harmful or offensive contact. Assault focuses on mental well-being, whereas battery is concerned with physical well-being.

Mnemonic: **Real Athletes In Heat Or Cold Intensely compete**

1. Reasonable Apprehension

a. Reasonableness
A reasonable person standard is used in determining the reasonableness of a plaintiff's apprehension. However, the minority view, as used in the Restatement, is that a defendant who has the requisite intent may commit an assault, regardless of whether the plaintiff's apprehension is reasonable.

b. Awareness
The plaintiff must have anticipated contact and known of the defendant's act in order to apprehend the contact.

Example:

Rob shoots at Susan and misses. Susan is unaware that Rob shot at her.

Result: Without awareness, there can be no apprehension and thus, no assault.

c. Apprehension Is Not the Same as Fear

A person who is aware that harmful or offensive contact will occur unless prevented may apprehend such contact, even if the person does not fear the contact.

2. Immediacy of Harmful or Offensive Contact

The harmful or offensive contact must appear imminent.

a. Future Harm

A threat of future harm, as opposed to imminent harm, may not constitute an assault.

b. Apparent Ability

A defendant must have the apparent ability to complete the act which the plaintiff apprehends.

c. Mere Words

Words alone are almost never sufficient to constitute an assault. Words must be accompanied by an overt act.

3. Intent

a. Two Types

A defendant's intent must fit one of two types:

i. Intent to cause apprehension, or

ii. Intent to commit a battery.

As in battery, the defendant need not intend harm.

b. Transferred Intent

The doctrine of transferred intent applies to assault. See Ch. 2, I, C.

B.   Damages
Damages may be awarded for the mental and physical effects of
an assault. Punitive and nominal damages may be awarded.

IV.   FALSE IMPRISONMENT

A.   Definition
False imprisonment is the intentional restraint of another to a
confined area.

1.   Intent
A defendant must have the intent to confine, or must act
despite substantial certainty that confinement will result.
Malice is not required and transferred intent applies.

2.   Restraint

a.   Physical Barriers, Force, or Threats
Restraint can be accomplished by physical barriers, force,
or threats against a person, property, or third parties.
Threats of future harm are insufficient to constitute
restraint, as are verbal commands unaccompanied by
threats or force.

b.   The Assertion of Legal Authority
If a person submits to restraint because of a reasonable
belief in another's asserted legal authority, there is a false
arrest and false imprisonment if the detainment is without
proper legal authority or cause.

3.   Confined Area
One must be restrained to a confined area. Mere obstruction
of passage is not false imprisonment.

B.   Awareness
The plaintiff must have either known of the confinement or
suffered some harm from it.

C. Escape
There can be no recovery for false imprisonment if the plaintiff had knowledge of a reasonable means of escape.

D. Duty to Release
False imprisonment occurs when a lawful confinement is unlawfully extended.

E. Damages
In addition to compensatory damages, nominal and punitive damages may be awarded. Recovery for mental suffering is permitted.

V. INTENTIONAL INFLICTION OF MENTAL DISTRESS

A. Definition
The intentional infliction of mental distress occurs when one intentionally or recklessly causes severe emotional damage to another through extreme and outrageous conduct.

1. Intent
A plaintiff must show that the defendant intended the infliction of distress, knew with substantial certainty that emotional distress would result, or acted with reckless disregard of a high probability that emotional distress would occur. Transferred intent does not generally apply. But see Ch. 4, I.

2. Severe Emotional Damage
A plaintiff's emotional damage must be severe; annoyance or hurt feelings are insufficient. If a reasonable person would not have suffered shock or severe damage from the defendant's conduct, the defendant is not liable. If a defendant acted with knowledge of a plaintiff's extra sensitivity, the defendant will be liable without regard to the reasonableness of the plaintiff's damages.

3. Extreme and Outrageous Conduct
Extreme and outrageous conduct is intentional conduct which exceeds all reasonable bounds of decency in a civilized society.

B. Damages
A plaintiff must prove actual, but not necessarily physical damages. Nominal damages are not awarded.

## VI. TRESPASS TO LAND

A. Definition
A trespass to land is the intentional invasion of another's interest in the exclusive possession of land. A person in constructive or actual possession of the land can assert this action.

B. Physical Invasion
A physical invasion to another's land occurs if a defendant:

1. Enters upon the land,

2. Causes another person or an object to enter the land,

3. Fails to remove something from the land which the defendant is under a legal duty to remove, or

4. Wrongfully remains on the land, despite a legal entry.

C. Intent

1. Traditional Rule
Trespass was traditionally a strict liability offense under English common law.

2. Modern Rule
One must intend to commit or cause the physical invasion of the plaintiff's land. No intent to harm is necessary. A reasonable, but mistaken belief that the land was one's own, or that the actor had a privilege to enter the land, is not a

defense to trespass. One need only to intend to step on the land.

D.  Damages
Nominal damages, as well as actual damages, may be recovered. A defendant is strictly liable for all consequential damages that naturally, directly and proximately result from the trespass.

## VII.  TRESPASS TO CHATTELS

A.  Definition
A trespass to chattel is the intentional interference with a chattel in someone else's possession. A person in constructive or actual possession of the chattel can assert this action.

B.  Chattel
Chattels are personal property, as opposed to real property.

C.  Act
One may commit trespass to chattel by either:

1. Damaging another's chattel, or

2. Dispossessing another of a chattel.

D.  Intent
Intent to do the act which is a trespass suffices. One does not have to show intent to harm. A mistake as to ownership is not a defense to trespass to chattels.

E.  Damages
Only actual damages, as opposed to nominal damages, may be recovered. Actual damages are presumed if possession is lost for any period of time. Because title never passes to the tortfeasor, the tortfeasor may return the chattel and pay reduced damages.

## VIII. CONVERSION

A.  Definition
    Conversion is interference with another's property that is so substantial that the original possessor loses title to the property and is entitled to full compensation.

    Examples of conversions:

    1. Improper possession (e.g., theft, embezzlement, fraud),

    2. Improper transfer of chattels (e.g., improper delivery, selling of stolen goods),

    3. Improper retention of chattels (e.g., refusal to return to rightful owner),

    4. Improper destruction or damaging of goods,

    5. Improper use (e.g., use without permission).

B.  Intent
    One must only intend to do the act that is adverse to another's right to possess the chattel. One does not have to intend harm.

C.  Property Subject to Conversion
    All tangible personal property and any physical documents that represent intangible property are subject to conversion.

D.  Factors Considered

    1. Dominion
       One's degree of control over the chattel.

    2. Good Faith
       An innocent mistake may prevent liability.

    3. Harm
       The amount of damage done to the chattel.

4. Inconvenience
The amount of inconvenience and expense caused the owner.

E. Damages
One whose property has been converted is entitled to the full value of the lost property.

Exception:
Replevin — If the actor who converted the property acted in good faith and the property is undamaged, the actor may mitigate damages by returning the property. Damages for loss of possession and inconvenience would still be awarded.

IX. CONSENT

Consent or permission relieves a defendant from liability. A plaintiff has the burden of proving that there was no consent. An exception to this is the tort of trespass to land.

A. Types of Consent

1. Express Consent
Express consent exists where a plaintiff directly states a willingness to accept a defendant's conduct.

2. Implied Consent
Implied consent exists where a plaintiff's behavior suggests consent to a defendant's actions. Consent may be implied in four major ways:

a. Objective Manifestation
Implied consent exists when a plaintiff's words or conduct are such that a reasonable person would interpret them to be consent. E.g., entering a crowded bus suggests consent to being shoved, which would otherwise be battery.

b. Subjective Manifestation
Implied consent may be shown from a plaintiff's actions toward a third party. E.g., Rob tells a third party that he

will let Susan play on his lawn, but he does not tell this to Susan. If Susan plays on Rob's lawn, no trespass has been committed.

 c. Implied by Law
  Consent is implied by law when it is in the best interest of a party, such as in emergency situations where one cannot consent for oneself. See Ch. 2, IX, D.

 d. Inaction
  A plaintiff's consent may be implied by inaction in certain situations.

**B.** Bars to Effective Consent
Even if consent is expressly given, it may be void under the following circumstances:

Mnemonic: **I'M FACED**

1. Incapacity
 Infants, drunkards, and mentally incompetent persons are incapable of giving consent. However, a person who is responsible for such an incapacitated person can consent for that person.

2. Mistake
 Consent mistakenly given by a plaintiff is generally valid. However, a mistake will negate consent if:

 a. The defendant knew of the plaintiff's mistake; or

 b. The defendant failed to warn the plaintiff of the inherent risks of the defendant's actions.

3. Fraud
 Consent induced by fraud is invalid if the fraud concerns an essential matter.

4. Act is Criminal

    a. Majority View
    Consent to a criminal or illegal act is invalid.

    b. Minority and Restatement (2d) View
    Even consent to a criminal or illegal act can be valid.

    c. Generally
    When a law is passed with the purpose of protecting a class of persons against their own judgment, consent by a member of the protected class is ineffective (e.g., a minor cannot consent to sexual intercourse).

5. Extreme Duress
Consent obtained under duress is invalid if the harm that was threatened was immediate; threat of a future harm will not negate consent.

C.    Scope
A defendant cannot exceed the limits of the actual consent given without being exposed to liability. An exception is made in emergency situations.

D.    Emergency Situations
A defendant can act without a plaintiff's consent if:

1. The plaintiff is unconscious or without the capacity to make a decision, and no one has been legally authorized to decide for the plaintiff;

2. Serious harm would result from a delay; or

3. A reasonable person would consent under the circumstances.

E.    Note
Consent usually applies only to intentional tort cases and not negligence. The equivalent to consent in the area of negligence is assumption of risk.

X.    SELF-DEFENSE

One is allowed to use reasonable force to defend against a threat of imminent harmful or offensive contact or the threat of confinement. The danger can be caused either intentionally or negligently.

A.    Reasonable Belief
The belief upon which one bases the need for self-defense must satisfy the reasonable person standard.

B.    Force

1. Reasonable Force
The minimum amount of force necessary to protect against a harm with which a person is faced.

2. Deadly Force
Can only be used when one is threatened with imminent death or serious bodily harm.

C.    Retreat
The majority rule is that there is no obligation to retreat from danger before resorting to self-defense.

D.    Third Party Injuries
When one accidentally injures a third party while justifiably using force in self-defense, there is no liability if one did not act recklessly, negligently, or intentionally.

XI.    DEFENSE OF OTHERS

The majority view is that one acting upon a reasonable belief in the protection of another may use the same amount of force that the person being defended would be entitled to use.

## XII.  DEFENSE OF PROPERTY

A.  Generally
One may use reasonable force to protect one's property after making a verbal demand that the invasion of the property be stopped.

B.  Limitations

1.  Reasonable Force
The minimum amount of force that would be necessary to protect the property. Only reasonable force can be used in the defense of property.

a.  Force may *not* be used to recapture property that has been permanently dispossessed.

b.  Deadly force may *only* be used to defend property under the following circumstances:

i.   When its use is necessary to prevent the burglary of a dwelling; or

ii.   When there is a threat to the safety of the defender.

2.  Verbal Demand
A verbal demand is not required if harm or violence will occur immediately, or if verbal requests will be useless.

3.  Mistake
A mistake may affect the validity of a use of force in defense of property.

a.  Mistake of Danger
If an owner mistakenly but reasonably believes the use of force is necessary, the use is privileged.

b. Mistake of Privilege
If an owner mistakenly believes that an intruder is a trespasser, but the intruder really has a privilege to trespass, the use of force is not privileged.

4. Booby Traps
The use of booby traps is privileged only up to the amount of force an owner would be allowed to use had the owner been present.

Exception: owners are never allowed to use a booby trap that causes death, even if they would have been allowed to use deadly force had they been present. The law prizes life over property.

## XIII. RECOVERY OF PROPERTY

A. Generally
A property owner can recover a chattel if the following elements are met:

Mnemonic: **FRUIT**

1. Force
Any force used must be reasonable and not deadly or capable of causing serious injury.

2. Right Wrongdoer
Force may only be used against the person who actually has the chattel. There is no privilege allowed for making a "reasonable mistake."

3. Unlawful Possession
The chattel must have been unlawfully taken.

4. In Hot Pursuit
An owner must be in hot pursuit of the taker. An owner cannot recover chattel by force after substantial time has elapsed.

5. Timely Oral Demand
There must be a timely oral demand to return the chattel before one may resort to force, unless such a demand would be futile or dangerous.

B.   Location of Chattel

1. On A Wrongdoer's Land
When an owner's chattel is on a wrongdoer's land, the owner can enter upon the land in a reasonable manner to recover the chattel.

2. On A Third Party's Land

a. Another's Fault
When a chattel is on a third party's land due to the fault of someone other than the owner of the chattel, the owner can enter in a reasonable and peaceful manner, even if the third party refuses entry. Nonetheless, the owner is liable for any damages caused.

b. Chattel Owner's Fault
When a chattel is on the land of another by the fault of the chattel owner, the chattel owner has no privilege to enter the land without permission.

C.   Shopkeepers
Shopkeepers have a privilege to temporarily detain persons who they reasonably believe have possession of "shoplifted" merchandise. Generally, this privilege is limited to the store's premises while the shoplifter is in the store. Some jurisdictions extend it to the area immediately outside the store.

## XIV. NECESSITY

A.   Generally
A party is privileged to interfere with another's property to avoid an injury threatened by some force of nature or from some independent cause not connected to the property owner.

1. Reasonably Apparent
The privilege of necessity exists as long as the necessity is "reasonably apparent," regardless of whether it actually exists; a reasonable mistake is allowed.

2. Resistance
A property owner cannot resist a party who has the privilege to enter under necessity.

B. Types of Necessity

1. Public Necessity
If a danger affects an entire community, or so many people that the public interest is at stake, a defendant has an absolute privilege to avert the peril and is not liable for damages. The privilege of public necessity is often extended to cases involving the media and free speech.

2. Private Necessity
If a danger affects only a person's personal interests, the harm to another's property interest is weighed against the severity and likelihood of the danger to determine whether the person has a privilege. Even with a privilege, the person still has to pay the other for the damages caused.

## XV. AUTHORITY OF LAW

Officers of the law and certain other people are privileged to make lawful arrests. They are not liable for any damage that results from the lawful arrest.

## XVI. DISCIPLINE

Parents, teachers and military superiors are privileged to use reasonable force in furtherance of their rightful duties.

## XVII. JUSTIFICATION IN GENERAL

Justification is a loosely defined "catch all" privilege.

## CASE CLIPS

### Ellis v. D'Angelo (1953) Ke
**Facts:** Ellis was pushed by D'Angelo, age four. She sued D'Angelo for battery and negligence and D'Angelo's parents for negligence because they knew of their child's propensity to attack others.
**Issue 1:** Can a minor formulate the intent needed for battery?
**Rule 1:** An infant tortfeasor is capable of having the intent to harm, and therefore can be liable as an adult.
**Issue 2:** Can a minor be negligent?
**Rule 2:** A minor may lack the mental capacity to be negligent.
**Issue 3:** Can a parent be found liable for failing to warn others of a child's violent propensities?
**Rule 3:** A parent is not vicariously liable for the torts of a child unless the parent's negligence made it possible for the child to cause the injury.

### Beauchamp v. Dow Chemical Co. (1986) Ke
**Facts:** Beauchamp brought an action against his employer alleging that the injury he suffered at his workplace was intentional.
**Issue:** Under what circumstances is a workplace injury considered to be an intentional tort by the employer?
**Rule:** Where an employer intended an act that injured an employee and knew that the injury was substantially certain to occur from the act, the employer has committed an intentional tort against the employee.

### Fisher v. Carrousel Motor Hotel, Inc. (1967) Ke
**Facts:** A plate was snatched from Fisher's hands by one of Carrousel Motor Hotel's employees while shouting "that no Negro could be served."
**Issue:** Is the intentional snatching of an object from a person's hands without touching or injuring the person's body a battery?
**Rule:** Knocking or snatching anything from a person's hand, or touching anything connected with the person in an offensive manner is an offense to the person's dignity and constitutes battery.

### Jones v. Fisher (1969) Ke
**Facts:** Fisher pulled out Jones' false teeth after Jones quit working for Fisher. Jones sued and recovered for emotional distress.
**Issue:** May a court modify a jury's award of damages?
**Rule:** A trial court can reduce the amount of compensatory or punitive damages.

### Mink v. University of Chicago (1978) Ke
**Facts:** Mink was treated with DES, an experimental drug, during her pregnancy. The treatment was without her knowledge.
**Issue:** Is it battery to administer treatment to a person who has not given consent?
**Rule:** Administering treatment without a patient's consent may be a battery. Hostile intent is not necessary.

### O'Brien v. Cunard Steamship Co. (1891) Ke
**Facts:** The defendant's doctor vaccinated O'Brien who was holding out her arm and waiting in a line to be examined for immunization. O'Brien sued for assault, but Cunard claimed that she had consented.
**Issue:** Must consent be verbal?
**Rule:** Silence and inaction when considered in connection with the surrounding circumstances may constitute consent to what would otherwise be an assault.

### Markley v. Whitman (1893) Ke
**Facts:** While walking home from school, the plaintiff was injured when the defendant was pushed into him by other students as part of a game. The plaintiff did not know about the game.
**Issue:** Are involuntary actions that occur during a possibly dangerous activity actionable if they cause an injury to a nonparticipant?
**Rule:** An actionable assault occurs when a nonparticipant is injured by persons engaged in a potentially dangerous activity. Participants in such an activity consent to the forms of the activity and thus are liable for even involuntary actions which are related to the activity.

### Elkington v. Foust (1980) Ke
**Facts:** Foust was accused of sexually abusing his minor daughter. He claimed her recovery of damages was barred because she consented.
**Issue:** Is consent by a minor a defense to a willful tort?

**Rule:**   To constitute a defense to a willful tort, consent must be given by one with legal capacity to consent. Minors are incapable of legally consenting to acts of sexual abuse.

### Kennedy v. Parrott (1956) Ke

**Facts:**  A surgeon discovered and removed a cyst on the plaintiff's ovary which led to complications during an authorized appendectomy.
**Issue:**   May a physician who finds an unexpected problem while doing an authorized procedure perform an unauthorized operation?
**Rule:**   Physicians may lawfully perform necessary operations so long as they stay within the area of the original incision and the patient (or the patient's representative) is incapable of giving consent.

### Fraguglia v. Sala (1936) Ke

**Facts:**  The plaintiff attacked the defendant with a pitchfork. In his defense, the defendant knocked the plaintiff down, causing injuries.
**Issue:**   How much force may a person use in self-defense?
**Rule:**   The amount of force allowed for self-defense is only that which is reasonably necessary to repel the attack. The question of what is reasonably necessary depends on the facts and circumstances of each case and how the circumstances appeared to the defendant. One is only liable for damages caused by excessive force.

### Dupre v. Maryland Management Corp. (1954) Ke

**Facts:**  The defendant struck Dupre and fractured his jaw after Dupre had assaulted him and threatened further assaults.
**Issue:**   Has excessive force been used when one's retaliatory blows result in a more serious injury than necessary to stall an attack?
**Rule:**   To assert that excessive force was used by one who acted in self-defense a plaintiff must prove that the defendant intended to inflict unnecessary injury.

### State v. Leidholm (1983) Ke

**Facts:**  Leidholm killed her sleeping husband after they had fought violently earlier in the evening. She claimed self-defense.
**Issue:**   What standard of reasonableness is used to determine whether deadly force in self-defense was justified?

**Rule:** To use deadly force in defending oneself a person must have a sincere and reasonable belief that the use of force was necessary to protect oneself from an imminent and unlawful harm.

### Commonwealth v. Drum (1868) Ke

**Facts:** After the plaintiff struck the defendant with his fists, the defendant stabbed and killed the plaintiff.

**Issue:** May one use deadly force in response to an unarmed attack?

**Rule:** One may kill another in self-defense only if it is reasonable to believe that the assailant is about to take one's life or cause great bodily harm, and there is no opportunity to escape.

### People v. Young (1962) Ke

**Facts:** Young aided a person being arrested by an undercover police officer.

**Issue:** Is one criminally liable for the mistaken but reasonable belief that one is protecting another from an unlawful attack?

**Rule:** The right of a person to defend another is as great as that person's right to defend oneself.

### Katko v. Briney (1971) Ke, Ep

**Facts:** Briney booby-trapped his boarded-up farmhouse with a spring gun to protect against trespassers. Katko was severely wounded when he entered Briney's house to steal fruit jars.

**Issue:** May a person protect one's property with deadly force?

**Rule:** A person may not take actions that would cause serious injury to another in defense of one's property.

### Kirby v. Foster (1891) Ke, Ep

**Facts:** Foster refused to give Kirby, his bookkeeper, a paycheck because Kirby could not account for missing funds. Kirby took money from the employees' payroll to reimburse himself. Foster used force to recover the money, injuring Kirby.

**Issue:** Can one use force to recover property?

**Rule:** The privilege of using force to recover one's personal property does not apply when the holder of the property lawfully obtained possession.

### I de S et Ux v. W de S (1348) Ke, Ep

**Facts:** W swung a hatchet at M, wife of I, but missed.

**Issue:** Is it a trespass to commit an assault which causes no harm?

**Rule:** An assault is a harm in itself for which one may recover damages, even if it is unaccompanied by other harm.

### Read v. Coker (1853) Ke

**Facts:** The defendant and his employees threatened to break the plaintiff's neck if he did not leave the premises.

**Issue:** Can threatening words constitute an assault?

**Rule:** Words alone do not amount to an assault. An assault is an attempt, coupled with present ability, to do personal violence to another.

### State Rubbish Collectors Ass'n v. Siliznoff (1952) Ke

**Facts:** The Association threatened to beat up Siliznoff, burn his truck, and destroy his business unless he joined the Association.

**Issue:** Can one be liable for inflicting severe emotional distress which is unaccompanied by physical injury?

**Rule:** One who, without privilege to do so, intentionally causes severe emotional distress to another is liable for such emotional distress, and for bodily harm resulting from it.

### Eckenrode v. Life of America Insurance Co. (1972) Ke

**Facts:** The defendants refused to pay the proceeds of Eckenrode's murdered husband's life insurance policy.

**Issue:** Under what circumstances does an intentional infliction of emotional distress occur?

**Rule:** The elements of intentional infliction of emotional distress are outrageous conduct, intent to cause or recklessly causing emotional distress, actual severe or extreme emotional distress, and proximate cause. The outrageous character of one's conduct is shown by an abuse of a position affecting the interest of another or knowledge of another's particular susceptibility.

### Whittaker v. Sandford (1912) Ke

**Facts:** Whittaker voluntarily boarded Sandford's yacht and sailed from Syria to Maine. On arrival, Sandford refused to furnish Whittaker with a small boat to go ashore.

**Issue:** Can one commit false imprisonment without using physical force?

**Rule:** One need not exert physical force to be liable for false imprisonment; actual physical restraint is sufficient.

### Teel v. May Department Stores Co. (1941) Ke

**Facts:** A department store detective confiscated goods that Teel had bought with a fraudulently obtained credit card, and detained her until she would sign a confession.

**Issue:** May a shopkeeper detain a person after illegally obtained goods are returned?

**Rule:** A suspected shoplifter may only be detained by a store owner until goods are recovered, innocence is determined, or police are notified.

### Zaslow v. Kroenert (1946) Ke

**Facts:** Kroenert removed Zaslow's furniture from a house they owned in common and put it in storage.

**Issue:** Is it a conversion to intermeddle with one's property?

**Rule:** Conversion occurs when there is a substantial interference with the possession or right to property. Intermeddling with, use of or damage to another's property is not conversion, though one may recover for impairment of the property or loss of its use in an action for trespass or case.

### Smith v. Stone (1648) Ke

**Facts:** A third party threw Stone onto Smith's land.

**Issue:** Is one who involuntarily enters the land of another guilty of trespass?

**Rule:** When one party forces a second party onto another's land, only the first party is liable for trespass.

### Gilbert v. Stone (1648) Ke

**Facts:** Stone entered Gilbert's house and took a horse because his life was threatened.

**Issue:** Are threats of violence a defense to a trespass action?

**Rule:** Threats of violence against an actor do not justify a trespass since the party whose land was trespassed upon has no other remedy than against the actor.

### Cleveland Park Club v. Perry (1960) Ke

**Facts:** Perry, age 9, caused serious damage by placing a tennis ball under a drain cover of the plaintiff's pool.

**Issue:** Must a child have the intent necessary to perform an act that caused a trespass?

**Rule:** A minor is capable of forming the intent necessary to commit the intentional tort of trespass.

### Wheat v. Freeman Coal Mining Corp. (1974) Ke

**Facts:** Wheat brought a nuisance action against the defendant, a coal mine, for emitting dust and smoke onto his property.

**Issue 1:** What are the elements of a nuisance action?

**Rule 1:** Nuisance is an injury that is caused by an intentional and unreasonable act, and is determined by weighing the gravity of injury against the utility of the conduct.

**Issue 2:** How are damages measured in a nuisance action?

**Rule 2:** The measure of damages in a nuisance action is the value of the discomfort and deprivation of the healthful use of the land.

### Nicholson v. Connecticut Half-Way House, Inc. (1966) Ke

**Facts:** The plaintiffs brought a nuisance action to prevent the Connecticut Half-Way House from using a house as a residence for paroled convicts.

**Issue:** Are fears of future harm sufficient to merit an injunction in apprehension of a possible nuisance?

**Rule:** No injunction should ever be granted merely because of the fears and apprehension of future harm.

### Monongahela Navigation Co. v. United States (S.Ct. 1893) Ke

**Facts:** The federal government condemned a dam. The defendant had a right to collect tolls from those passing through the dam.

**Issue:** What compensation must the government provide to an owner of property when the government has condemned the property?

**Rule:** (Brewer, J.) Upon exercise of its right to condemn property, the federal government must provide "just compensation" which includes both the commercial value of the property as well as its intangible value.

### Harrison v. Wisdom (1872) Ke

**Facts:** The defendants destroyed all the liquor in their town, including the plaintiff's, to prevent an approaching Federal army from getting drunk and demolishing the town.

**Issue:** Is one personally liable for destroying the property of another if it is done for the good of the public?

**Rule:** There is no liability for the destruction of another's property if an impending and imminent peril makes it absolutely necessary. The destruction only needs to appear necessary at the time it is done.

### Ploof v. Putnam (1908) Ke, Ep

**Facts:** While sailing with his family, the plaintiff was forced to moor his boat to the defendant's dock when a sudden storm developed. The defendant untied the boat, causing damage.

**Issue:** Can a property owner eject a trespasser who is using the property for refuge?

**Rule:** The privilege of private necessity, which allows one to use another's property to avoid serious injury, may not be defeated by the property owner.

### Vincent v. Lake Erie Transportation Co. (1910) Ke, Ep, Fr

**Facts:** The plaintiff's vessel was kept docked during a severe storm, causing damage to the dock.

**Issue:** Must a party who asserts private necessity as a defense to the invasion of another's property compensate the owner of the property for the resulting damage?

**Rule:** While private necessity permits the invasion of another's property, the invader remains liable for resulting damages.

### Crescent Mining Co. v. Silver King Mining Co. (1898) Ke

**Facts:** Silver King built a pipeline across Crescent's land without causing any damage. Crescent sought an injunction and damages.

**Issue:** Can one recover damages for a harmless intrusion on one's property?

**Rule:** A harmless intrusion on one's land is compensated by nominal damages.

### Tuberville v. Savage (1669) Ep

**Facts:** The plaintiff put his hand on his sword and said, "If it were not assize-time, I would not take such language from you."

**Issue:** Can a threatening gesture constitute an assault?

**Rule:** A threatening gesture does not constitute an assault when accompanying words indicate that there will be no attempt at contact.

### Vosburg v. Putney (1891) Ep

**Facts:** One student lightly kicked the leg of another student during class, intending no harm. The leg was sensitive from a previous injury and was severely damaged by the kick.

**Issue:** Is proof of intent to harm required to recover damages for assault and battery?

**Rule:** Intent to harm is not an element of battery. Only proof of intent to commit an unlawful act or proof of fault is necessary.

### Mohr v. Williams (1905) Ep

**Facts:** During surgery on the plaintiff's right ear, Williams, a doctor, discovered that the left ear was in worse condition and operated on it. The plaintiff had only consented to the right ear operation, and there was no emergency to perform the operation on the left ear.

**Issue:** Can a physician who discovers unexpected conditions during a consensual operation perform the necessary additional procedures?

**Rule:** A physician commits battery by performing a procedure which is different from the authorized procedure, unless the condition endangers the life or health of the patient.

### Hudson v. Craft (1949) Ep

**Facts:** The plaintiff was injured by an opponent's blow in a boxing match at a carnival. The prize fight violated a state statute.

**Issue:** Can people forfeit their rights to sue under tort law by consenting to a violation of a statute written for their protection?

**Rule:** Members of a class cannot waive a right created by statute to protect their class.

### McGuire v. Almy (1937) Ep

**Facts:** An insane person injured her caretaker-nurse.

**Issue:** May an insane person be held liable for an intentional tort?

**Rule:** An insane person who intentionally causes damage will be held liable. The insane person will not be excused even if a peculiar mental condition caused the person to entertain the intent.

### Courvoisier v. Raymond (1896) Ep

**Facts:** Courvoisier shot a police officer whom he erroneously thought was one of several persons attacking him.

**Issue:** May a defendant assert self-defense if the person who was injured did not attack the defendant?

**Rule:** Use of force may be justified as self-defense if the defendant reasonably believed there was a threat of a great harm and the actions taken were necessary to prevent such perceived harm.

### McIlvoy v. Cockran (1820) Ep

**Facts:** McIlvoy severely wounded Cockran because he was tearing McIlvoy's fence down.

**Issue:** May one use deadly force to protect one's property?

**Rule:** One may not inflict severe injury to protect property unless a trespasser is committing a violent felony or endangering human life.

### Bird v. Holbrook (1825) Ep

**Facts:** The plaintiff was injured when he tripped a spring gun which the defendant had set to protect a flower garden.

**Issue:** May property be protected with devices that can cause serious injury?

**Rule:** Devices that cause serious injury may not be used to protect property unless sufficient warnings are posted.

### Alcorn v. Mitchell (1872) Ep

**Facts:** The defendant spat upon the plaintiff.

**Issue:** May punitive damages be awarded without pecuniary loss?

**Rule:** Punitive damages may be awarded when malice, willfulness, wantonness, outrage, and indignity attend the wrong, regardless of the loss suffered.

### Bird v. Jones (1845) Ep

**Facts:** The defendant enclosed part of a public highway so spectators would have to pay him to watch a boat race. The plaintiff was prevented from advancing within the enclosed area.

**Issue:** Can partial obstruction constitute false imprisonment?
**Rule:** Partial obstruction does not constitute confinement for purposes of false imprisonment.

### Coblyn v. Kennedy's Inc. (1971) Ep

**Facts:** Coblyn was held on an erroneous suspicion of shoplifting.
**Issue:** Is it false imprisonment to detain someone inaccurately suspected of committing a crime?
**Rule:** Any general restraint or demonstration of physical power that can be avoided only by submission constitutes false imprisonment. However, shopkeepers may detain persons they reasonably suspect of shoplifting in a reasonable manner for a reasonable period of time.

### Wilkinson v. Downton (1897) Ep

**Facts:** The defendant, as a practical joke, told the plaintiff that her husband had broken both legs in an accident. The plaintiff went into "nervous shock" with accompanying physical effects.
**Issue:** Does a cause of action arise from malicious words that result in physical injury?
**Rule:** Intentional, extreme, and malicious conduct causing mental and physical distress gives rise to a valid cause of action.

### Bouillon v. Laclede Gaslight Co. (1910) Ep

**Facts:** The defendant engaged in a rude conversation with the plaintiff's nurse and blocked the doorway with his hand. The plaintiff was frightened and suffered a miscarriage.
**Issue:** Is one liable for injuries resulting directly and naturally from one's wrongful conduct?
**Rule:** Fright and mental anguish are competent elements of damage and if physical injury results from such fright, compensation is merited.

### George v. Jordan Marsh Co. (1971) Ep

**Facts:** Jordan Marsh repeatedly harassed the plaintiff to pay her son's debt.
**Issue:** May harassment create a compensable cause of action for emotional distress?
**Rule:** One who, without privilege, intentionally causes severe emotional distress by extreme and outrageous conduct is subject to liability if bodily harm results from such distress.

### Hustler Magazine v. Falwell (S.Ct. 1988) Ep, Fr

**Facts:**  Falwell, a well known minister, was the subject of a parody in Hustler Magazine that falsely described his first sexual encounter.

**Issue:**  Must a public figure prove "actual malice" to recover for intentional infliction of emotional distress?

**Rule:**  (Rehnquist, C.J.)  To recover for the intentional infliction of emotional distress a public figure must prove actual malice.

### Garratt v. Dailey (1955) Fr

**Facts:**  Dailey, age 5, pulled a chair from under Garratt knowing she was about to sit down.

**Issue:**  May one be liable for battery without an intent to harm?

**Rule:**  The "intent" element of battery is fulfilled if one knew with "substantial certainty" that contact would occur.

### Lopez v. Winchell's Donut House (1984) Fr

**Facts:**  The Donut House suspected Lopez, an employee, of pocketing sales money. Lopez voluntarily came to the Donut House at the request of her employer, and remained in a room of the shop to clear her name. No force or threats were used to detain Lopez, and she left the room when she began to feel ill.

**Issue:**  Does a false imprisonment occur if one is compelled to remain in a place to protect one's reputation?

**Rule:**  Remaining in a place to clear one's name does not constitute false imprisonment. For a false imprisonment to occur, the plaintiff must have yielded to force, a threat of force (implied or express), economic duress or the assertion of authority.

### Womack v. Eldridge (1974) Fr

**Facts:**  Eldridge intentionally and recklessly obtained Womack's photograph for presentation at a criminal trial that Womack had no real connection with. After the presentation, the plaintiff had to appear in court numerous times, and was suspected of committing a crime. The ordeal caused the plaintiff serious emotional distress that was not accompanied by physical injury.

**Issue:**  Is one who intentionally or recklessly causes severe emotional distress to another by extreme and outrageous conduct subject to liability for such emotional distress absent any bodily injury?

**Rule:**   An action will lie for emotional distress unaccompanied by bodily injury if (1) the wrongdoer's conduct was reckless or intentional, (2) the conduct was outrageous such that it went against accepted standards of decency and morality, (3) the conduct caused the plaintiff's emotional distress, and (4) the emotional distress was severe.

### Owen v. City of Independence (S.Ct. 1980) Fr

**Facts:**   Owen, a police chief, was fired without the benefit of a hearing. The defendant had acted in good faith in denying the hearing because the constitutional right to have a "name clearing" hearing was only recognized after the plaintiff was fired.

**Issue:**   Can a municipality violate a person's civil rights in good faith without incurring liability?

**Rule:**   (Brennan, J.)   A municipality is liable for violations of civil rights even if the municipality acted in good faith.

**Dissent:**   (Powell, J.)   Municipalities should not be held strictly liable for violations of constitutional rights. If a municipality acted in good faith when denying the right, it should be immune from liability.

# Chapter 3

## NEGLIGENCE

### I.    GENERALLY

Negligence is an unintentional tort, meaning that a defendant may be liable absent an intent to commit the tort. A plaintiff has to show that the defendant's behavior created an unreasonable risk of harm to others by departing from a reasonable standard of care, and that it was the proximate cause of the plaintiff's damages.

### II.    ELEMENTS OF CAUSE OF ACTION

Mnemonic: **Don't Be Careless Dummy**

A.    **D**uty to use reasonable care to conform to a standard of conduct so as to avoid unreasonable risks to others. It is necessary to establish that the defendant had a duty to the *specific* plaintiff not to create an unreasonable risk. See *Palsgraf v. Long Island R.R. Co.*

B.    **B**reach of the Duty.

C.    **C**ausation
The breach of the duty must be the proximate cause of the plaintiff's harm.

D.    Actual **D**amages
Actual damages must be shown; one may not recover for nominal damages.

### III.    UNREASONABLE RISK OF HARM

In deciding whether a defendant caused an unreasonable risk of harm, the courts will look at several issues:

A.    Foreseeability
Something is foreseeable if there is a significant likelihood of its occurring. No person is expected to guard against causing harm that is completely unforeseeable, or harm that is so unlikely as to be commonly disregarded.

B.    Balancing Test
Using Judge Learned Hand's formula, liability will result when $B < L \times P$, where:

$B$ = The defendant's Burden to avoid/prevent the risk.
$L$ = Gravity of the injury or Loss.
$P$ = Probability that an injury (loss) will occur.

Thus, one who is deciding whether to take a precaution so as to lower the risk of harm to others should weigh the cost of taking the precaution (B) against the probability (P) that an injury will occur if the precaution is not taken multiplied by the gravity of the loss (L).

C.    Utility of Conduct
The court will look to the social utility of creating a risk when determining if the creation of the risk is unreasonable.

Example:
Though the probability of grave injury from automobile accidents is high, we will not deem the mere use of an automobile negligent since the use of cars has an extremely high social utility.

IV.    STANDARD OF CARE

A.    Generally
A defendant's conduct is measured against a certain standard of care to determine if the defendant actually breached a duty, i.e., failed to meet the requirements of that standard.

B.  Reasonable Person
The reasonable person standard is an objective standard. The relevant inquiry is how a reasonable person under the same circumstances as the defendant would have acted, as opposed to whether the defendant acted according to a personal notion regarding proper conduct.

1. Intoxication
Intoxication is not an excuse for unreasonable conduct.

2. Exceptions

a. Children
Children are held to the standard of a reasonable child of similar age, intelligence, etc. However, the reasonable child standard is not used if the child is engaged in an adult activity.

b. Physical Attributes or Handicap
One is held to the standard of a reasonable person with one's physical attributes or handicaps.

c. Mental Capacity

i.  Slight Mental Deficiency
One must act as a reasonable person of average mental ability. There is no excuse for a slight mental deficiency.

ii.  Extremely Low Intelligence
For example, a moron or an imbecile. The majority view is that such a person is not capable of being negligent.

iii.  Insanity
Insane persons are generally held to a reasonable person standard. The rationale is to encourage guardians to supervise their insane wards, to avoid false claims, and to make the party who actually caused the

loss responsible. However, a few courts have held that an insane person who is not capable of appreciating or avoiding danger is not negligent.

    iv.  Sudden Illness or Unconsciousness
For example, a seizure or delirium. One is not liable for the consequences of a sudden illness or unconsciousness if the sudden lapse was completely unforeseeable.

### 3. Knowledge
One is assumed to have the knowledge of a reasonable person of ordinary experience.

  a.  Strangers
Strangers and newcomers to a community are assumed to know all the facts specific to that area which all the adults of that community know.

  b.  Investigation
In some instances one may have a duty to remedy one's ignorance by conducting a reasonable investigation, even if people of the community share the same ignorance.

## C.  Professionals
Professionals such as doctors, lawyers and accountants are liable if they do not meet the minimum standards of their professions.

### 1. Locality Rule
Generally, professionals are required to follow the standards of their profession as practiced by other members in the same locality. The more modern view is that a professional should be judged according to a uniform national standard, especially with regard to professions where there is nationwide uniformity in certification.

2. Success Is Not Guaranteed
   There is no requirement that a professional succeed for a client, only that the professional act with the requisite amount of skill.

3. Differing Schools of Thought
   When opinions in a profession may reasonably differ, a professional can choose any reasonably accepted school of thought.

4. Specialists
   Specialists are held to a higher standard than professionals without a specialty.

5. Novices
   Newly licensed professionals are held to the same standard as experienced members of the profession.

6. Unreasonable Standard
   If a court rules that a professional standard is inherently negligent, then professionals who follow the standard are also negligent.

7. Doctrine of Informed Consent
   Physicians must inform patients of risks that are inherent in medical procedures, unless the treatment is given in an emergency situation and the patient is incapable of giving consent.

D.  Custom and Usage
    Custom and Usage are the general practices of a particular community or industry within society, such as the medical profession or the mining industry.

1. Generally
   In general, a defendant who has conformed with a custom may introduce such conformity as evidence of reasonable care. However, custom is not conclusive as to what is proper behavior.

2. Abandonment of Custom
Failure to adhere to a custom is irrelevant if one uses ordinary and reasonable care.

E. Aggravated Negligence
Some states have defined various degrees of negligence, such as gross negligence, recklessness, and willful and wanton conduct, in the context of automobile guest statutes.

1. Automobile Guest Statutes
Automobile guest statutes generally provide that a nonpaying passenger can only sue the car's driver if the driver was grossly negligent or acted with willful misconduct.

2. Rationale
The rationale behind automobile guest statutes is to prevent collusion between the driver and the passenger.

3. Constitutionality
Numerous state supreme courts have held automobile guest statutes as violative of state or federal constitutions. Few states still require aggravated negligence for liability to guests.

V. RULES OF LAW

Though negligence is generally a question for the jury, courts sometimes set out standards of behavior. These standards are usually, but not always, adopted by other courts.

VI. VIOLATION OF STATUTES

In some cases, the appropriate standard of conduct is determined by a statute, e.g., speed limits, drinking laws. An unexcused violation of a statute by a defendant resulting in injury to the plaintiff will invoke liability. In such cases, the usual negligence standards of the reasonable person are superseded by the more stringent standards set by the statute.

A.  Applicability
    A statute is applicable to prove liability if:

    Mnemonic: **Could Have Stopped**

    1. **C**lass
       The plaintiff is part of the class of persons the statute is intended to protect,

    2. **H**arm
       The harm suffered by the plaintiff is the type that the statute is intended to prevent,

    3. **S**tandard
       The required standard of conduct is clearly defined in the statute.

B.  Excuse
    Violation of a statutory duty is excused if:

    1. Compliance would be more dangerous than noncompliance,

    2. Compliance is impossible, or

    3. The defendant was faced with an emergency he did not create.

C.  Criminal Liability
    A statutory violation immediately invokes criminal liability.

D.  Civil Liability

    1. Majority View
       A statutory violation is negligence per se.

    2. Minority View
       A statutory violation is only some evidence of negligence that may be outweighed by other evidence showing due care.

3. Statutory Reference
If the statute explicitly states that its violation gives rise to civil liability, then even the minority will impose liability.

E. Obsolete Statutes
A court will often ignore evidence of a statutory violation if the statute has not been enforced for a long time, or if it is without foundation.

## VII. PROOF OF NEGLIGENCE

A. Circumstantial Evidence
Circumstantial evidence is evidence of one fact from which another fact may be inferred. It can be used to show that a defendant breached the duty of care. Drawing inferences from circumstantial evidence, however, is highly prejudicial to a defendant who has the burden of rebutting the inference. Therefore, courts will carefully regulate its use.

B. Expert Testimony
A plaintiff in a malpractice suit must produce expert testimony unless the negligence is obvious to a lay person (e.g., doctor amputated wrong leg).

C. Res Ipsa Loquitur
Res ipsa loquitur means roughly that "the thing speaks for itself." This is the classic use of circumstantial evidence in torts. Under this doctrine, a plaintiff can create an inference or presumption of negligence against the defendant by the mere fact of the accident having occurred.

1. Elements

Mnemonic: **OPEC**

a. **O**rdinarily an accident of that nature would not have occurred unless someone was negligent.

b. **P**laintiff was free from fault.

c. Exclusive Control
   The defendant exercised exclusive control over the instrumentality that caused the injury.

Note: Recent cases indicate that courts require only a preponderance standard (51% probability) for each element.

2. Procedure
   Once the plaintiff has asserted res ipsa loquitur, the defendant is allowed to rebut with evidence tending to show the use of due care.

   a. Majority View
      Res ipsa loquitur creates an *inference* of negligence from which a reasonable jury may conclude that the defendant was negligent. The plaintiff, however, cannot get a directed verdict even if the defendant does not introduce rebutting evidence.

   b. Minority View
      Res ipsa loquitur creates a *presumption* of negligence which entitles the plaintiff to a directed verdict if the defendant does not rebut.

3. Multiple Defendants
   Res Ipsa can be applied to two or more defendants even though only one was negligent if they were all involved with activities surrounding the injury and it is difficult to pinpoint the person who actually caused the injury.

## CASE CLIPS

**The Case of the Thorns (1466) Ke, Ep**
**Facts:** When the defendant trimmed his hedges, some thorns fell on the plaintiff's property. The defendant entered the plaintiff's property to remove the thorns, whereupon the plaintiff asserted an action for trespass.

**Issue:** Is one liable for damages resulting from an innocent act?
**Rule:** One who voluntarily commits an act that results in damages to another will be responsible for the damages, even if the act was lawful.

### Weaver v. Ward (1616) Ke, Ep

**Facts:** Ward accidentally fired his gun during war games, injuring Weaver.
**Issue:** Does an accidental injury give rise to liability?
**Rule:** A party is liable for the results of its actions, unless the party is utterly without fault.

### Brown v. Kendall (1850) Ke, Ep, Fr

**Facts:** The plaintiff's dog and the defendant's dog were fighting. The defendant repeatedly struck the dogs with a stick to separate them, but accidentally hit the plaintiff in the eye.
**Issue:** Is there liability for assault and battery for injuries that are inadvertent and unintentional?
**Rule:** One is liable for damages resulting from actions conducted in an unlawful, intentional, or negligent manner.

### Butterfield v. Forrester (1809) Ke

**Facts:** The plaintiff was thrown from his horse when the horse hit a pole left in the road by the defendant. The plaintiff was riding very fast and evidence suggested that the pole could have been seen from 100 yards away.
**Issue:** May a defendant's negligence be excused by a plaintiff's failure to exercise ordinary care?
**Rule:** A plaintiff is barred from recovering damages caused by another's negligence when the exercise of ordinary care by the plaintiff could have prevented the accident.

### The Nitro-Glycerine Case (S.Ct. 1872) Ke

**Facts:** The defendant, a common carrier, transported an unmarked box containing a new experimental chemical. The defendant did not make inquiries as to its contents. When the box leaked, the defendant attempted to open it, causing an explosion that destroyed the plaintiff's nearby building.

**Issue:** What degree of care must a person exercise in order to avoid liability for negligence?

**Rule:** (Field, J.) A person must take the precautions that a reasonable person, guided by considerations which ordinarily regulate the conduct of human affairs, would take. One who exercises reasonable care will not be liable for unintentional injuries.

### Fletcher v. Rylands Ke, Ep

**Facts:** The defendant had a reservoir constructed close to the plaintiff's coal mines. When the reservoir filled, water broke through an abandoned mine shaft and flooded the plaintiff's mines. Though the contractors and engineers were negligent, the defendant was not personally negligent.

**Issue:** May a person be liable for damages caused despite the use of due care?

**In the Exchequer (1865):**

**Rule:** Unless damages are immediate, there can be no trespass. Unless the act is unlawful, there can be no nuisance. Unless there is negligence, there can be no liability.

**In the Exchequer Chamber (1866):**

**Rule:** One who brings *anything* on land which is likely to do mischief if it escapes is strictly liable for damages which are the natural consequence of its escape.

**In the House of Lords (1868):**

**Rule:** One is strictly liable for damages resulting from the dangerous *non-natural* use of land.

### Losee v. Buchanan (1873) Ke

**Facts:** The defendant's boiler exploded, damaging the plaintiff's property. The plaintiff did not allege that the defendant was negligent in any way.

**Issue:** Is one who nonnegligently causes damage liable?

**Rule:** One who is free of fault, intent or negligence is not liable for damages.

### Van Skike v. Zussman (1974) Ke

**Facts:** Van Skike, a minor, obtained a toy cigarette lighter as a prize from a gum ball machine in Zussman's store. He immediately purchased lighter fluid from Zussman and accidentally set himself on fire.

**Issue:** Is a defendant negligent for allowing a minor to come into possession of a remotely dangerous article?

**Rule:** A defendant who supplies a minor with a remotely dangerous article will only be negligent if the harm or danger caused by the article is reasonably foreseeable, as opposed to merely possible.

### Davis v. Consolidated Rail Corp. (1986) Ke

**Facts:** One of Davis' legs and part of his foot were severed from his body when a train he was inspecting was moved without warning.

**Issue:** Will the absence of safety precautions invariably result in the imposition of liability?

**Rule:** A defendant who fails to take a safety precaution is liable for negligence only if the burden (B) of taking the precaution is less than the magnitude of the potential loss (L) multiplied by the probability (P) of the accident occurring (i.e., $B < PL$).

### Beatty v. Central Iowa Railway (1882) Ke

**Facts:** The defendant placed a railroad track in close proximity to a public highway. Beatty was killed when the approach of a train caused his horse to become unmanageable and run into the train.

**Issue:** Is a party who could have avoided the occurrence of an accident negligent?

**Rule:** A party is negligent only if it did not use reasonable care and diligence, in light of the existing circumstances, to guard against danger.

### Vaughan v. Menlove (1837) Ke, Ep

**Facts:** Menlove stacked hay on the edge of his property near Vaughan's cottages in such a manner that the hay was likely to ignite. Menlove was warned by many people of the risk of fire but thought it best to "chance it."

**Issue:** Does the required standard of care involve acting to the "best of one's judgement" or with such reasonable caution as a prudent person under such circumstances?

**Rule:** Negligence is not determined by the subjective standard of one's own judgement but by the objective reasonable person standard.

### La Marra v. Adam (1949) Ke

**Facts:** A police car carrying a premature baby to a hospital drove through a red light at 45 miles per hour without using a siren. The plaintiff collided with the police car.

**Issue:** Does conduct involving a high probability of hurting someone constitute recklessness or negligence?

**Rule:** Recklessness implies conscious appreciation of the probable extent of danger or risk incident to a contemplated action, while negligence in the legal sense implies knowledge only of a probable source of danger in the act.

**Note:** This is the minority rule (distinguishing between recklessness and negligence). Most states would likely hold the officer negligent based on the theory that a reasonable person would exercise extra caution in more dangerous situations.

### Whicher v. Phinney (1942) Ke

**Facts:** The defendant drove behind another car which struck a wagon, causing the plaintiff to be ejected from the wagon. When the defendant became aware of the dangerous situation ahead he only had time to act instinctively, and ran over the plaintiff.

**Issue:** Is it possible for one who is acting according to instinct to be negligent?

**Rule:** An act committed when there is only a short time to act is called an instinctive action. A party who has not negligently caused an emergency situation and who has acted instinctively is not negligent, unless the party was unfit to act in an emergency.

### Public Service of New Hampshire v. Elliott (1941) Ke

**Facts:** Elliott, an electrical construction student, was electrocuted because he came too close to a high tension wire when he pointed to a piece of machinery in the defendant's electrical substation.

**Issue:** Is a spontaneous and natural gesture that results in injury a contributorily negligent action if the person making the gesture has special knowledge of the danger?

**Rule:** A reasonable person may make a spontaneous movement without analyzing all of the ramifications. In such a case, the standard to be used is that of a reasonable person in like circumstances, e.g., what a reasonable student of electricity would do.

### Smith v. Sneller (1942) Ke

**Facts:** Smith, a man with very poor eyesight, fell into a trench dug by Sneller.

**Issue:** Is it contributorily negligent for a blind person to walk alone in a public area without a cane or other special precautions?

**Rule:** It is not negligence for a blind person to walk alone in public areas, but the blind person must conform with the standard of ordinary prudence (i.e., a reasonable blind person would have used a cane).

### Williamson v. Garland (1966) Ke

**Facts:** An 11 year old was injured when his bicycle was struck by an automobile.

**Issue:** Is a minor capable of negligence?

**Rule:** A minor who does not exercise the degree of care reasonably expected from a child of like age and experience may be negligent.

### Wright v. Tate (1967) Ke

**Facts:** Wright, an adult with low mental capacity, was killed while riding in a car driven by an intoxicated person. Tate charged that Wright was contributorily negligent for riding in the car when he knew the driver was intoxicated.

**Issue:** What standard of care should apply to determine the contributory negligence of a person of low intelligence?

**Rule:** One who has a mental deficiency which falls short of insanity is held to the same standard of reasonable care as a person of greater or normal intelligence.

### Breunig v. American Family Ins. Co. (1970) Ke, Ep

**Facts:** The defendant was overcome by a sudden mental delusion, causing her to crash into Breunig's oncoming truck.

**Issue:** Is insanity a defense to a negligence action?

**Rule:** While insanity is generally not a defense to negligence, it is a valid defense where the actor, without forewarning, is overcome by a mentally disabling disorder. The defense for sudden mental incapacity is analogous to the defenses for sudden heart attack or epileptic seizure.

### Titus v. Bradford, B. & K. R.R. (1890) Ke, Ep

**Facts:** The Bradford, B. & K. Railroad followed a common industry practice of removing broad gauge boxcars from their wheel assemblies and setting them on narrow gauge assemblies. In the process, a boxcar tipped off its wheel assembly and killed Titus.

**Issue:** Does following the custom and usage of a trade or business satisfy the requirement of exercising a reasonable standard of care?

**Rule:** The test for negligence is whether a defendant's methods, machinery, and appliances comport with the ordinary usage of the business or trade.

### The T.J. Hooper (1932) Ke, Ep

**Facts:** The defendant's tugboats and the barges they towed sunk during a storm. The tugs did not have radios capable of transmitting warning of the storm. It was not common to equip tugboats with radios at the time.

**Issue:** Does following a common custom and usage satisfy the obligation to exercise the proper duty of care?

**Rule:** The common practice of a profession is relevant but not conclusive in determining one's use of due care. The practice itself may be unreasonable and negligent according to common knowledge and the judgment of a prudent and reasonable person.

### Rossell v. Volkswagen of America (1985) Ke

**Facts:** Rossell's Volkswagen rolled over in an accident. The battery, which was inside the passenger compartment, fractured and leaked sulfuric acid, disfiguring Rossell.

**Issue:** In negligent design cases, are product manufacturers held to an expert's standard of care?

**Rule:** In determining what is reasonable care for manufacturers, a plaintiff need only prove that the defendant's conduct presented an unreasonable risk of harm. As in all other negligence cases, the jury is permitted to decide what is reasonable according to common experience.

### Bly v. Rhoads (1976) Ke

**Facts:** The plaintiff sued her doctor after adverse complications arose from a hysterectomy, claiming that her physician did not comply with the informed consent doctrine. The plaintiff introduced an expert who was unfamiliar with local community medical standards.

**Issue 1:** May lay testimony as to a "patient's need" for information be used to determine what information a physician must disclose?

**Rule 1:** A plaintiff must produce an expert to establish the prevailing medical practice with respect to the disclosure of information to patients, that the information was material to an informed decision, and that disclosure would not have posed an unreasonable threat to the patient's well-being.

**Issue 2:** Is familiarity with the local community medical standards required of an expert giving testimony in a malpractice suit?

**Rule 2:** An expert must have knowledge of a same or similar community standard in order to testify in a malpractice action.

### Helling v. Carey (1974) Ke, Ep

**Facts:** Helling's eye was permanently damaged because Carey failed to diagnose her glaucoma. Experts for both parties agreed that standards of the specialty did not require an exam for glaucoma for patients below the age of forty. Helling was under forty.

**Issue:** Does compliance with the professional standards of a specialty satisfy the appropriate duty of care?

**Rule:** Professionals whose actions conform to the standards of their given specialty may, nevertheless, commit malpractice if such conduct is not reasonably prudent.

### Martin v. Herzog (1920) Ke, Ep, Fr

**Facts:** Martin was killed when his buggy was struck by Herzog's car. Herzog alleged that Martin was contributorily negligent by driving without lights, contrary to a safety statute.

**Issue:** Is violation of a safety statute evidence of contributory negligence?

**Rule:** Unexcused omission of a statutory requirement is more than evidence of negligence, it is negligence per se which cannot be nullified by a jury. However, it must be shown that such omission contributed to the damages in order to be contributory negligence.

### Tedla v. Ellman (1939) Ke, Fr

**Facts:** The plaintiffs were struck by the defendant's negligently driven automobile. The defendant claimed that the plaintiffs were contributorily negligent for failing to obey a statute requiring pedestrians to walk facing oncoming traffic.

**Issue:** Is violation of a safety statute negligence per se?

**Rule:** Violation of a safety statute may be excused if a greater risk of harm would have resulted from complying with the statute.

### Bauman v. Crawford (1985) Ke

**Facts:** While riding his bicycle after dark, the plaintiff, aged fourteen, was injured in a collision with the defendant's car. Contrary to a statute, the plaintiff's bicycle lacked a headlight.

**Issue:** Is the negligence per se doctrine applicable to minors?

**Rule:** A minor's statutory violation is not negligence per se, but may be introduced as evidence of a minor's negligence. The minor is negligent only if the jury finds that a reasonable child of the same age, intelligence, maturity and experience would not have acted in violation of the statute under the circumstances.

### Zerby v. Warren (1973) Ke

**Facts:** The plaintiff, age 14, died after sniffing glue that his friend, also a minor, purchased from Warren. Warren asserted the defenses of contributory negligence and assumption of the risk. A statute prohibited the sale of glue to minors.

**Issue:** Does violating a child protection statute create absolute liability on the part of a retailer for the wrongful death of a minor which resulted from an intentional act?

**Rule:** Liability for the violation of a statute designed to protect a child is absolute. Therefore, defenses such as contributory negligence and assumption of the risk are inapplicable.

### Thompson v. Frankus (1955) Ke

**Facts:** The plaintiff was injured when she fell down the defendant's poorly maintained and unlit stairway. The plaintiff was not sure of the cause of her fall.

**Issue:** Can a plaintiff who is unaware of the specific cause of injury sue for negligence?

**Rule:** A plaintiff who is unable to recount or explain an accident may nevertheless recover if the deficiency is met by other direct or circumstantial evidence.

### Newing v. Cheatham (1975) Ke, Fr

**Facts:** The plaintiff was killed when the defendant's plane crashed. The cause of the crash could not be determined.

**Issue:** What must be established to assert a negligence action based on res ipsa loquitur?

**Rule:** The doctrine of res ipsa loquitur may be invoked when: (1) the accident is of a kind which ordinarily does not occur in the absence of negligence; (2) the accident is caused by an instrumentality within the exclusive control of the defendant; and (3) the plaintiff is free from fault.

### Sutor v. Rogotzke (1972) Ke

**Facts:** A hunter accidentally fired his gun, killing the plaintiff.

**Issue:** Does the doctrine of res ipsa loquitur apply to accidental injuries caused by dangerous instrumentalities?

**Rule:** In cases involving dangerous instrumentalities, res ipsa loquitur is applicable.

**Note:** This case represents the majority view.

### Ybarra v. Spangard (1944) Ke, Ep, Fr

**Facts:** Asserting res ipsa loquitur, Ybarra sued his surgeon and other hospital staff after suffering paralysis of his shoulder and arm following an operation to remove his appendix.

**Issue:** May the doctrine of res ipsa loquitur be applied against several defendants when there is no showing of who specifically caused the injury and when no particular defendant ever had exclusive control over the plaintiff?

**Rule:** The doctrine of res ipsa loquitur will apply to all those defendants who had any control over the plaintiff's body or the instrumentalities which might have caused the injuries to the plaintiff. It is up to each defendant to rebut the presumption of negligence.

**Note:** This case illustrates the "smoking out of the evidence" policy used when members of the same profession will not testify against each other.

### Scott v. Shepherd (1773) Ep

**Facts:** Shepherd threw a lit explosive into a marketplace. Several persons threw the device away from themselves to avoid injury. Scott lost an eye when he was struck by the explosive.

**Issue:** Is an originator of mischief relieved of liability due to the presence of intervening parties?

**Rule:** One is liable for injuries which result from unlawful, deliberate, indiscriminate, and wanton mischief despite the intervening conduct of other parties acting under a compulsive necessity for their own safety and self-preservation.

### Brown v. Collins (1873) Ep

**Facts:** The defendant's horses became frightened and unmanageable, damaging the plaintiff's property. The defendant exercised ordinary skill and care in managing his horses.

**Issue:** Is a party liable for damages caused by its property if the party was not negligent and did not act improperly?

**Rule:** Liability is not imposed for a force set in motion that damages the property of another unless the plaintiff can show fault or negligence.

### Powell v. Fall (1880) Ep

**Facts:** Fall's tractor, operating in a lawful manner and without mechanical defect, emitted a spark that caused Powell's hay to catch fire.

**Issue:** Is a party liable for damages caused by its potentially dangerous activity without any negligence or fault?

**Rule:** A party who conducts a dangerous activity is liable for damages caused regardless of fault or negligence.

### Louisville Ry. Co. v. Sweeney (1914) Ep

**Facts:** Defendant's trolley car jumped from its tracks and hit a telephone pole. The telephone pole hit a gate which struck Sweeney who was standing in her front yard.

**Issue:** Is negligence required to effect a trespass?

**Rule:** A defendant's action need not be negligent in order to be a trespass. One who trespasses upon another or sets a force in motion which causes trespass upon another is liable unless the trespass is caused by an act of God or forces beyond the defendant's control.

### Stone v. Bolton (1950)
### Bolton v. Stone (1951) Ep

**Facts:** As Stone passed outside some cricket grounds she was struck by a cricket ball that Bolton hit. The cricket grounds were quite large and were surrounded by a fence. Only six to ten balls had ever been hit outside the grounds in 30 years.

**Issue:** Is one liable for failing to protect against an extremely unlikely, but foreseeable risk?

**Rule:** There is no liability for a foreseeable injury that is not caused by negligence or an intentional action if the known risk of the injury is extremely minimal.

**Note:** Some courts will find liability if precautions were easily available and inexpensive.

### Hammontree v. Jenner (1971) Ep

**Facts:** Jenner had a past history of epileptic seizures. After 14 years without a seizure, one occurred causing him to have a car accident in which Hammontree was injured. Jenner had a valid driver's license and the authorities knew of his condition.

**Issue:** Is there strict liability for accidents occurring due to sudden forces beyond a defendant's control?

**Rule:** An accident caused by a force outside one's control will not lead to liability. However, if the person knew or should have known that the uncontrollable force was likely to come on suddenly, the person's conduct may be negligent.

### Roberts v. Ring (1919) Ep

**Facts:** The plaintiff, a seven year old boy, was struck by the defendant's automobile while crossing the street. The defendant was a seventy-seven year old man with defective sight and hearing.

**Issue:** Is it proper to consider one's age, maturity or infirmities when determining negligence or contributory negligence?

**Rule:** Negligence is judged by the standard of care usually exercised by the ordinarily prudent normal person, while contributory negligence is judged by the standard of care commonly exercised by an ordinary person in the actor's position, taking into account factors such as age and maturity.

### Daniels v. Evans (1966) Ep

**Facts:** Daniels, age 19, was killed when his motorcycle struck Evans' automobile. The trial court instructed the jury that because Daniels was a minor he should have exercised the care of the average child of his age and experience and should not be held to the same standard as an adult.

**Issue:** Is a minor engaged in an adult activity held to the same standard of care as an adult?

**Rule:** When a minor undertakes an adult activity which can result in grave danger to others and to the minor, the minor should be held to the standard of a reasonable adult.

### Fletcher v. City of Aberdeen (1959) Ep

**Facts:** Barriers surrounding a ditch were negligently removed. Fletcher, a blind man walking with a cane, fell in the ditch and suffered injuries.

**Issue:** Does a keeper of public property have a duty to prevent injury to disabled people who might use the property?

**Rule:** The disabled have a right to use public property. Thus, keepers of public property must anticipate its use by disabled people and take necessary precautions to prevent them from being injured.

### Robinson v. Pioche, Bayerque and Co. (1855) Ep

**Facts:** Robinson, drunk, fell into a hole in a public street that Pioche, Bayerque and Co. left uncovered.

**Issue:** Does one owe a lesser duty of care to an intoxicated person?

**Rule:** Intoxication of a plaintiff cannot excuse a defendant's gross negligence.

### Denver & Rio Grande R.R. v. Peterson (1902) Ep

**Facts:** Peterson, a warehouse worker, was charged with negligence, because he did not take adequate precautions to protect the plaintiff's property.

**Issue:** Is the required standard of care modified by the defendant's income level?

**Rule:** The required standard of care is not affected by a person's financial standing.

### Smith v. Lampe (1933) Ep

**Facts:** Smith, hearing a boat coming to shore at the wrong place on a foggy night, drove his car to the shore and blew his horn to warn the captain. Lampe mistook Smith's horn for a pre-arranged safe passage signal, and crashed his boat on the rocks.

**Issue:** Is one liable for innocent actions that result in unforeseeable injury?

**Rule:** One is not liable for unforeseeable injuries resulting from non-negligent conduct.

### Blyth v. Birmingham Waterworks Co. (1856) Ep

**Facts:** Blyth's house was damaged when a fire hydrant, installed by Birmingham, sprung a leak due to a severe and unusual frost. The hydrant had worked properly for 25 years prior to the incident.

**Issue:** Is it negligence to fail to plan for a rare and extraordinary situation?

**Rule:** Negligence involves the omission of an action that a reasonable person would perform, or acting in a way that a prudent and reasonable person would not.

### Eckert v. Long Island R.R. (1871) Ep

**Facts:** Eckert was struck by the defendant's negligently operated train when he saved a child who was sitting on the tracks.

**Issue:** Is it negligent to place one's life in danger to save the life of another?

**Rule:** Risking one's life for the purpose of saving another is not wrongful, and therefore, not negligent, unless it was either rash or reckless.

### Hauser v. Chicago, R.I.& P. Ry. (1928) Ep

**Facts:** Hauser severely burned her face when she fainted and fell against an exposed steam pipe in the bathroom on a train.

**Issue:** Must a property owner anticipate and take precautions to prevent injuries to others who use the property in an unusual manner?

**Rule:** A party who takes reasonable precautions for the ordinary and safe use of its property is not liable for an injury that it could not have anticipated.

## Osborne v. Montgomery (1931) Ep

**Facts:** The plaintiff was injured when his bicycle crashed into the partly opened door of the defendant's double parked car.

**Issue:** Is all conduct that creates risk to others considered below the required standard of ordinary care?

**Rule:** Social value should be balanced against the degree of risk to determine the question of negligence. A reasonable amount of risk which naturally flows from socially acceptable and desirable conduct has to be tolerated.

## Cooley v. Public Service Co. (1940) Ep

**Facts:** The defendant's power line fell during a storm, causing a loud noise to pass through the plaintiff's phone while she was using it. The plaintiff suffered psychological and physical injuries. The only way to prevent the risk of such noises would involve changes to the wires that would greatly increase the risk of electrocution to pedestrians.

**Issue:** If one cannot simultaneously protect against two kinds of harm, is one negligent to only protect against the more serious and likely harm?

**Rule:** When only one of two harms can be protected against, efforts should be made to protect against the more serious and likely harm.

## United States v. Carroll Towing Co. (1947) Ep, Fr

**Facts:** Plaintiff's barge broke away from a pier and sunk due to the defendant's negligence in shifting its mooring lines and the plaintiff's contributory negligence in not having an employee on board to prevent such an accident.

**Issue:** Has a party breached its duty of care when it could have avoided a tremendous risk with a relatively minimal amount of effort?

**Rule:** A party is liable for negligence when the burden (B) of adequate precautions is less than the probability (P) of the injury causing event times the possible gravity of injury (L). (B < PL)

## Mayhew v. Sullivan Mining Co. (1884) Ep

**Facts:** Mayhew, a mine worker of Sullivan Mining, fell into an unlit and unguarded ladder hole in the mine. Sullivan tried to introduce evidence that it was an industry custom to cut such holes.

**Issue:** Is the standard of care determined by the custom of an industry?

**Rule:**   Reasonableness, and not custom, determines the standard of care. A custom which, on its face, is inconsistent with ordinary care or a due regard for safety is properly excluded as evidence of due care.

### The T.J. Hooper (1931) Ep

**Facts:**   The defendant's tugboats and the barges towed by the tugboats were lost in a storm. The tugboats did not have working radios to warn them of the storm. Ninety percent of the other tugboats operating on the coastline were equipped with working radios.

**Issue:**   Does a common custom and industry practice impart a duty on an actor in the profession to conform with that custom?

**Rule:**   A reasonable and prudent professional has a duty to conform with the universal practices or customs of an industry.

**Note:**   This is the trial court decision of the case found on page 65.

### Brune v. Belinkoff (1968) Ep

**Facts:**   Brune fell down eleven hours after Belinkoff injected her with a spinal anesthetic. In response to an allegation that the dosage was excessive, Belinkoff claimed the dosage was customary in New Bedford, Massachusetts, even though lower dosages were used in Boston and New York.

**Issue:**   Should a local or national standard be used to determine a physician's duty of care?

**Rule:**   The locality rule is abandoned; physicians are to be held to one national standard.

### Canterbury v. Spence (1972) Ep

**Facts:**   Canterbury sued Spence, a physician, for failing to provide adequate information and warning concerning a medical procedure after complications from a spinal operation resulted in partial paralysis.

**Issue:**   Is a doctor required to explain the risks inherent in a medical procedure when the custom of the profession is not to do so?

**Rule:**   A physician must disclose the likelihood and possibility of complications to a patient before performing a procedure.

### Anonymous (1703) Ep

**Facts:**   None given.

**Issue:** None given.
**Rule:** Wherever a statute enacts anything, or prohibits anything, for the advantage of any person, that person shall have a remedy to recover the advantage given him by the statute or damages for injury inflicted contrary to the statute.

### Osborne v. McMasters (1889) Ep

**Facts:** McMasters sold an unlabeled bottle of deadly poison to the plaintiff, in violation of a labeling statute. The plaintiff accidentally drank the poison and died.
**Issue:** Does a statutorily defined duty of care supersede the common law standard?
**Rule:** When a duty of care is established by statute, the common law duty to act with reasonable care is superseded so that violation of the statute constitutes conclusive evidence of negligence.

### Brown v. Shyne (1926) Ep

**Facts:** Brown was paralyzed by Shyne's chiropractic treatment. Shyne practiced medicine without a license, in violation of a state statute.
**Issue:** Is violation of a statute negligence per se if the statute was not intended to protect the public from the party in violation?
**Rule:** If a statute is not intended to protect against certain proscribed conduct, but rather against such conduct by a certain class of people, a violation of the statute by one who is not part of the regulated class is not negligence per se. Such a violation is not the proximate cause of an injury against which protection is afforded.

### Ross v. Hartman (1943) Ep

**Facts:** Hartman violated a traffic ordinance by leaving his truck unattended, unlocked, and with its keys in the ignition in a public alley. A thief stole the truck and negligently struck Ross.
**Issue:** Is one liable for damages resulting from the violation of an ordinance if the actual damages were caused by an intervening party?
**Rule:** Violation of an ordinance intended to promote public safety is negligence and is the legal and proximate cause of harm if the violation creates the hazard which the ordinance was intended to prevent.

### Vesely v. Sager (1971) Ep

**Facts:** Sager, in violation of a state statute, served a large quantity of alcoholic beverages to a customer who he knew was excessively intoxicated. As a result of intoxication, the customer negligently injured Vesely in a car accident. At the time the beverages were served, Sager also knew that the customer would be driving after consumption of the beverages.

**Issue:** Can negligent conduct be the proximate cause of an injury if there is intervening action by a third person between the negligent conduct and the injury caused?

**Rule:** If negligent conduct is a substantial factor in bringing about an injury, and the intervening causes of the injury are reasonably foreseeable or normal incidents of the risk created, the negligent conduct may be deemed the proximate cause of the injury.

### Baltimore and Ohio R.R. v. Goodman (S.Ct. 1927) Ep, Fr

**Facts:** Goodman drove across the defendant's railroad tracks without stopping. He did not see the approaching train because it was obscured by a house. Goodman died in the collision.

**Issue:** May a judge establish a standard of appropriate conduct?

**Rule:** (Holmes, J.) While the question of due care is generally left to the jury, if the court is dealing with a standard of conduct and the standard is clear, it should be laid down by the court.

### Pokora v. Wabash Ry. Co. (S.Ct. 1934) Ep, Fr

**Facts:** Pokora was hit by a train after he failed to get out of his car at a railroad track crossing to look for oncoming trains, as was required under B. & O. R. Co. v. Goodman. It was unclear whether a prudent person under the circumstances would have adhered to the Goodman standard.

**Issue:** Is non-compliance with a given standard of care determinative of negligence?

**Rule:** (Cardozo, J.) Extraordinary situations may not wisely or fairly be subjected to tests or regulations that are fitting for the commonplace or normal. If a person determines that adherence to a given standard is unwise, one is not negligent by law for such deviation, but rather is subject to the judgment of a jury.

### Wilkerson v. McCarthy (S.Ct. 1949) Ep
**Facts:** The plaintiff slipped and fell while walking on an oily wood plank that traversed a ditch. The defendant had taken precautions to fence off the ditch.
**Issue:** Can a judge direct a verdict for a defendant even though there was sufficient evidence for a jury to lawfully rule in favor of the plaintiff?
**Rule:** (Black, J.) A judge may not direct a verdict when a jury could reasonably rule in favor of the opposite party.

### Byrne v. Boadle (1863) Ep, Fr
**Facts:** As he walked on a public street, Byrne was struck by a barrel of flour that fell out of a window of Boadle's shop.
**Issue:** Can the mere occurrence of an accident provide a presumption of negligence even though no other evidence of negligence is offered?
**Rule:** The doctrine of res ipsa loquitur provides that the mere fact of an accident having occurred is evidence of a defendant's negligence. A plaintiff is not bound to show the accident could not happen without negligence. If there are any facts inconsistent with negligence, it is for the defendant to prove them.

### McGonigal v. Gearhart Industries, Inc. (1986) Ep
**Facts:** McGonigal was seriously injured when he threw a defective hand grenade which was assembled and inspected by the defendant, Day & Zimmerman.
**Issue:** Must a plaintiff foreclose all possible nonnegligent causes of an accident in order to employ res ipsa loquitur?
**Rule:** A plaintiff is not required to eliminate with certainty all possible nonnegligent causes of the accident, but rather need only show that on the whole it is more likely than not that the asserted negligence was the cause of the accident.

### Colmenares Vivas v. Sun Alliance Insurance Co. (1986) Ep
**Facts:** The plaintiffs were injured when the handrail of a moving escalator stopped moving. Although the Puerto Rico Ports Authority owned the escalator and controlled the public area in which it was found, it contracted with another party to inspect, maintain and repair the escalator.

**Issue:** Is it necessary for a party to have exclusive physical control over an instrumentality which causes an accident in order to apply res ipsa loquitur against the party?

**Rule:** If a defendant has an nondelegable duty to maintain an instrumentality in a safe condition, it is ultimately responsible for the instrumentality and effectively has exclusive control over it. Unless the duty is delegable, the res ipsa loquitur inference is not defeated if the defendant shifts physical control to an agent or contracts with another to carry out its responsibilities.

### Dillon v. Legg (1968) Ep

**Facts:** Dillon suffered great emotional injury when she saw her daughter killed by Legg's negligent driving. Her safety was at no time endangered.

**Issue:** Can one recover for emotional trauma caused by witnessing the death of a close relative if one does not fear for his own safety?

**Rule:** In an action for emotional distress, factors such as proximity to the "zone of danger" and the relationship to the physically injured party may be considered in allowing for recovery.

### Molien v. Kaiser Foundation Hospitals (1980) Ep

**Facts:** The defendant erroneously diagnosed Molien as having syphilis. As a result, his wife divorced him.

**Issue:** Can one recover damages for the negligent infliction of emotional distress?

**Rule:** Even without physical harm, damages may be awarded for negligent infliction of emotional distress if the trier of fact is convinced of the genuineness of the claim in light of the circumstances.

### Adams v. Bullock (1919) Fr

**Facts:** The plaintiff was electrocuted when the eight foot long wire he was carrying struck the overhead wire for the defendant's trolley.

**Issue:** Must a party take every possible precaution to protect the welfare of others?

**Rule:** A duty exists to adopt all reasonable precautions to minimize possible perils. A party is not negligent for not providing protection against an unforeseeable, extraordinary injury that would be extremely difficult to prevent.

### Trimarco v. Klein (1982) Fr

**Facts:** Trimarco was injured when his bathtub's door enclosure shattered. He sued for negligence asserting that the manufacturer should have made the door from the tempered safety glass used throughout the industry.

**Issue:** Is reasonableness determined by the custom and usage of one's trade?

**Rule:** The custom and usage of a profession or trade is one factor in deciding the reasonableness of conduct. The reasonableness of the custom itself need also be considered.

### Negri v. Stop and Shop, Inc. (1985) Fr

**Facts:** Negri slipped and fell in the defendant's store. The floor was covered with broken jars and spilled food. The evidence showed that the food was dirty, one witness had not heard any jars break within the twenty minutes prior to the accident, and the floor had been cleaned between fifty minutes and two hours before the accident.

**Issue:** Is circumstantial evidence that a party should have known a dangerous condition existed on its property enough to establish a prima facie case of negligence?

**Rule:** A prima facie case of negligence may be established by circumstantial evidence that a party did not act to remedy a potentially hazardous condition of which the party had constructive notice.

### Gordon v. American Museum of Natural History (1986) Fr

**Facts:** Gordon fell down a museum's steps after slipping on a piece of waxy paper that came from the museum's concession stand.

**Issue:** What constitutes constructive notice of a dangerous situation for the purpose of establishing negligence on the basis of circumstantial evidence?

**Rule:** To be liable for negligence under the theory of constructive notice, a defect must be visible and apparent, and it must exist for a sufficient length of time to permit the defendant to discover and remedy it.

### Henning v. Thomas (1988) Fr

**Facts:** The defendants, Henning and Pruner, questioned on appeal the qualification of the plaintiff's expert to testify about the standard of care in Virginia, and the trial court's limitation on testimony concerning the expert's salary and relationship with the plaintiff.

**Issue 1:** May the determination of an expert's qualification to testify be overturned on appeal?

**Rule 1:** The question of whether an expert is qualified to testify rests largely within the sound discretion of the trial court. The decision to allow an expert to testify will not be reversed unless it clearly appears that the witness was unqualified.

**Issue 2:** Is testimony as to an expert's salary and relationship to the controversy admissible to establish bias and prejudice?

**Rule 2:** A court must permit a party to explore an expert's relationship to the plaintiff in order to allow the party to establish bias and prejudice.

### Pauscher v. Iowa Methodist Medical Center (1987) Fr

**Facts:** Pauscher died after the defendants performed a medical procedure without informing her of the risks involved.

**Issue:** If a physician withholds information from a patient to obtain the patient's consent to a medical procedure, must the patient suing for malpractice produce expert testimony establishing that the physician's nondisclosure was a deviation from professional standards?

**Rule:** Because the physician's duty to disclose is governed by each patient's need for particular information as opposed to professional standards, a patient is not required to prove that a physician's withholding of information was a deviation from professional standards. Rather, a physician who withholds information must assert a defense justifying the nondisclosure.

# Chapter 4

## THE DUTY OF CARE

### I. GENERALLY

As part of the cause of action for negligence, the plaintiff must show that the defendant actually had a duty not to expose the plaintiff to an unreasonable risk.

One of the issues that requires further examination is how far the duty extends. This chapter explores whether one has a duty to avoid causing mental disturbance to another, whether one has an affirmative duty to act, whether there is a duty to unborn children, and whether parties to a contract have a duty to parties not in privity.

### II. MENTAL DISTURBANCE AND RESULTING INJURY

It is difficult for plaintiffs to recover damages for mental suffering which is unaccompanied by physical injury. The reluctance to grant recovery is due to the difficulty in proving emotional damage in the absence of physical proof, the fear of excessive and fraudulent claims, and an absence of precedent.

#### A. Physical Impact Rule
If a plaintiff was actually hit and injured by a defendant, the courts will allow recovery for mental suffering which naturally follows from the impact as a "parasitic" damage.

#### B. Emotional Injury without Physical Impact

1. Majority View
   In the absence of a physical impact, the majority of jurisdictions will only allow recovery for mental distress if it is accompanied by physical symptoms.

   Exception: Recovery for pure emotional distress that is unaccompanied by physical symptoms is allowed in extreme cases such as the mishandling of a corpse or the misdiagnosis of a serious illness.

2. Minority View

A minority of courts allow recovery for the negligent infliction of emotional distress in the absence of physical impact or physical symptoms where the facts are such that a reasonable jury could believe that the emotional distress was genuine.

C.    Physical Injury without Physical Impact

The majority view is that a plaintiff can recover for physical injuries that result from emotional distress even if there was no physical impact.

D.    Fear for the Safety of Others

1. "Zone of Danger" Rule

Some jurisdictions will not allow recovery for emotional distress caused by the fear for another's safety, unless the plaintiff's safety was imperiled as well. That is, the plaintiff must have been within the "zone of danger" in order to recover, even if the emotional distress was accompanied by physical symptoms.

2. Other View

Some states have abandoned the "zone of danger" rule and will allow recovery depending on:

a.  How near the plaintiff was to the place of the accident,

b.  Whether the plaintiff directly witnessed the accident, and

c.  Whether the plaintiff was closely related to the injured party.

III. FAILURE TO ACT

A. Generally
There is generally no duty to act for the benefit of another if one has not created the risk.

B. Exceptions
There are certain situations where one has an affirmative duty to act such that liability will be imposed for failing to act.

Mnemonic: <u>SAP</u>

1. <u>S</u>pecial Relationship

   a. Between Defendant and Plaintiff
   If the defendant has a special relationship with the plaintiff such as parent-child, husband-wife or hospital-patient, there is an affirmative duty to act on the plaintiff's behalf. This category also covers innkeepers, common carriers and other business relationships.

   b. Between Defendant and Third Party
   In certain cases the defendant may have a special relationship with a third party that places a duty on the defendant to control that party or prevent that party from harming others.

   Example:
   The relationship between a psychiatrist and a patient imparts a duty on the psychiatrist to warn a party to whom the patient poses an immediate threat of serious harm. See *Tarasoff v. Regents of Univ. of California.*

2. <u>A</u>ssumption of Duty
   One who is not under a duty to act but does so anyway must proceed with reasonable care, and cannot leave an injured party if doing so would leave the party in worse condition than when assistance began.

Note: A physician who helps on the scene is only liable for "gross negligence."

3. Peril Caused by Defendant
If the defendant either negligently or innocently puts the plaintiff in danger, the defendant has a duty to help.

## IV. UNBORN CHILDREN

A. At Common Law
At common law, one did not owe a duty to an unborn child. For example, a child born with defects that were caused while still in the womb could not sue the responsible party for damages.

B. Recently
Over the past 40 years, some courts have modified the common law view by allowing recovery for damages caused while one was still in the womb in one of two situations:

1. Viable Fetus
Some courts require that there be a viable fetus at the time that the injury occurred. Some courts have considered a fetus that was a few weeks old to be viable.

2. Born Alive
Some courts require that the child be born alive.

C. Wrongful Life
A suit brought by a plaintiff against those people responsible for the plaintiff's birth. Courts have generally rejected such suits on the theory that one cannot argue that he was better off not being born. These suits are most likely to be allowed for congenital defects which, if properly diagnosed during a mother's pregnancy, would have led her to abort. Usually plaintiffs recover for medical expenses and sometimes for mental and emotional suffering.

## V.    PRIVITY OF CONTRACT

A.    Nonfeasance
Nonfeasance is the failure to perform a contractual promise.

1.  Parties to the Contract
    One party to a contract may sue another party to the contract for nonfeasance under contract law, but not under tort law.

    Exception: Common carriers and public utilities are liable in tort even when a contract exists.

2.  Third Parties
    One who is not a party to a contract may not sue a party to the contract for nonfeasance under contract law or tort law.

    Exception: A third party beneficiary of a contract may sue a party to a contract for nonfeasance under contract law.

B.    Misfeasance
Misfeasance of a contract is the improper performance of a duty under the contract.

1.  Parties to the Contract
    A party to a contract may recover for another party's misfeasance under either contract law or tort law.

2.  Third Parties
    Modern courts have not usually required a party to be in privity to a contract in order to recover in tort. For example, a third party may recover in tort from a manufacturer of a defective good even if the good was purchased from a dealer.

    Exception: A party who has not contracted with an attorney may not sue the attorney for misfeasance unless the party is an intended beneficiary of the contract.

## VI.   LANDOWNERS

At common law, an owner or occupier of land had a much lower duty of care to avoid causing an unreasonable risk of harm to others from the use of the land.

A.   Outside the Premises

1. Natural Hazards Located On the Property
Landowners do not have a duty to protect persons outside their land from natural hazards on their land.

Exception: Persons in densely populated areas must protect a public road from trees on their property.

2. Artificial Hazards Located On the Property
Landowners have a duty to protect persons outside their land from an unreasonably dangerous risk of harm.

B.   On the Premises
There are three types of persons who come onto a landowner's property: trespassers, licensees, and invitees. The owner's duty of care to each type of visitor is different. Some states (led by California and New York) have rejected the various categories of visitors in favor of requiring a landowner to exercise a standard of reasonable care to all of them.

1. Invitees

a. Two Types

i.   Business Visitors
Business visitors are persons invited by the owner onto the property to conduct business with the owner.

ii.   Public Invitees
Public invitees are persons who enter property that is open to the public for their own use.

b. Duty of an Owner
An owner has a duty to exercise ordinary care in keeping the property safe. The owner has a duty to inspect the property for unknown dangers.

c. Exceptions
Persons who exceed the scope of an invitation onto the property will void their status as invitees.

2. Licensees

a. Definition
Licensees are persons who enter an owner's property with the owner's consent, e.g., social guests. Firefighters and police officers are usually considered to be licensees.

b. Duty of an Owner
An owner does not have a duty to inspect the property for unknown dangers, but does have a duty to warn a licensee of any dangerous conditions of which the owner is aware.

c. Exceptions
Owners have a duty to exercise reasonable care when they are involved in "active operations of their land."

3. Trespassers

a. Undiscovered Trespassers

i. Definition
Persons who enter the property of an owner without permission or privilege.

ii. Duty of an Owner
An owner owes no duty to an undiscovered trespasser.

iii.   Exceptions
If an owner knows that trespassers frequent a limited portion of the property, the owner has a duty to warn of the dangers the trespassers would otherwise not discover.

b.  Discovered Trespassers

i. Definition
A particular person who an owner knows or should know is trespassing on the owner's property.

ii. Duty of an Owner
An owner must exercise reasonable care for the person's safety and warn of any dangers unknown to the person, but known to the owner.

While courts agree this is the standard for artificial conditions on the land, the courts are divided as to whether this standard applies to natural conditions.

c.  Child Trespassers

i.   Definition
Traditionally, a child had to be lured onto the property by an artificial hazard for an owner to be liable, i.e., the "attractive nuisance doctrine."

Under the modern view, a child-plaintiff must prove:

Mnemonic: **FRED**

(1)   Frequenting of the area by children is common and the owner knows of their tendency to enter the property.

(2)  **R**isks that the children are unable to appreciate makes the condition likely to cause injury; their ability to appreciate the risk is decided by a subjective standard.

(3)  **E**xpense of protecting against the injury is slight compared to the risk.

(4)  **D**angerous conditions are present that the owner knows of or should know of.

   ii.  Duty of an Owner
An owner must exercise reasonable care to avoid risks of harm from conditions that are artificial. An owner does not have a duty to protect against natural conditions.

C.  Lessor and Lessee

  1. Duties of a Lessee of Real Estate

    a. Liable for all damages caused on the property as an owner would be.

    b. Not liable for any harm caused in common areas.

  2. Duties of Lessor of Real Estate

    a. Generally, liability is passed from a lessor to a lessee.

    Exceptions:

     i.  A lessor is liable for a defect present at the start of a lease which the lessor knows or should know of, and that a lessee has no reason to know of. This does not mean the lessor has a duty to inspect, but rather a duty to warn.

ii.   A lessor is liable if the lessor knows the property will be open to the public and a defect exists when a lessee takes possession. A lessor in this case has a duty to inspect.

iii.   A lessor is liable for any damages that result from an act the lessor voluntarily performs that is done in a negligent manner.

iv.   A lessor is liable for a negligently repaired defect that the lessor is required to repair in the lease.

v.   A lessor is liable for damages which result from the lessor's improper maintenance of common areas.

b.   A lessor's duty is to the lessee and the lessee's guests and licensees.

D.   Vendors of Land
Generally, vendors of land are not liable for harm caused by defects on the land after it is sold.

Exceptions:

1. A vendor is liable for concealing a defect that the vendor knew the buyer would not find.

2. A vendor that did not conceal a defect is still liable until the buyer has had a reasonable time to discover and correct the defect.

### CASE CLIPS

**Rex v. Smith (1826) Ke**
**Facts:**  The defendants kept their mentally retarded brother in a cold and dirty room without a window.

**Issue:** Is there a duty to act on behalf of a sibling unable to care for one's own welfare?

**Rule:** Siblings living in their parents' home do not owe each other a duty of care.

### Hurley v. Eddingfield (1901) Ke

**Facts:** The defendant, a physician, refused to respond when a messenger told him that the plaintiff was violently ill and that no other doctor was available.

**Issue:** Must a physician assist any person requiring treatment?

**Rule:** A physician is not required to treat every patient who has requested medical services.

### Union Pacific Railway v. Cappier (1903) Ke

**Facts:** Though the railroad had operated its train with due care, it struck and killed Cappier's trespassing son. The train operator did not stop the train to give immediate medical attention to Cappier's son, but summoned an ambulance which arrived 30 minutes later.

**Issue:** Does a party who nonnegligently injured another party have a duty to rescue the injured party?

**Rule:** There is no obligation to rescue a stranger from peril that is life threatening peril where the defendant has not caused the peril.

### L.S. Ayres & Co. v. Hicks (1942) Ke

**Facts:** Hicks fell and caught his fingers in the defendant's escalator. The injury was aggravated by the defendant's slow reaction to the emergency.

**Issue:** Is there a duty to rescue a person in peril?

**Rule:** An actor has an affirmative legal duty to rescue a person in peril when the actor is an invitor, or when the injury resulted from an instrumentality under the actor's control.

### Szabo v. Pennsylvania Railroad (1945) Ke

**Facts:** The defendant failed to assist Szabo, its employee, when he was overcome by heat.

**Issue:** Does an employer have a duty to assist a sick employee?

**Rule:** If an employee engaged in the work of its employer receives injuries, the employer must render assistance regardless of whether the injuries are a result of the employer's negligence.

### Soldano v. O'Daniels (1983) Ke

**Facts:**  Soldano was murdered in a bar. A patron seeking to avert the murder tried to call the police at another public establishment, but was refused permission to use the telephone.

**Issue:**  Is there a duty to come to the aid of another?

**Rule:**  Although citizens are not generally required to aid a person in danger, an owner of a public establishment may not impede a person who has chosen to summon aid within that establishment.

### Thomas v. Winchester (1852) Ke

**Facts:**  The defendant, a druggist, bought falsely labeled poison from the manufacturer and sold it to the plaintiff, who suffered injuries.

**Issue:**  Is a manufacturer liable in negligence to an ultimate user who did not purchase directly from the manufacturer?

**Rule:**  A manufacturer does not owe a duty to an ultimate user. A party is liable only to the person with whom the party contracted.

### Ward v. Morehead City Sea Food Co. (1916) Ke

**Facts:**  The defendant sold spoiled fish to a grocer, who sold it to the plaintiff. The plaintiff died from eating the fish.

**Issue:**  Is one selling infected food liable to an ultimate consumer who purchased the food from an intermediary?

**Rule:**  One who sells food owes a duty of care to the ultimate consumer of the food.

### Paubel v. Hitz (1936) Ke

**Facts:**  The plaintiff slipped on the sidewalk outside the defendant's place of business. Both parties knew that the sidewalk was slippery.

**Issue:**  Are landowners required to warn an invitee of conditions which are obvious and known to the invitee?

**Rule:**  Landowners owe an invitee a duty to maintain their premises so they are reasonably safe and to warn of unsafe conditions only if they are neither obvious nor known to the invitee.

### Basso v. Miller (1976) Ke

**Facts:**  Basso, riding on the back of Miller's motorcycle, was injured in an accident caused by potholes in a public park. Basso sued Miller and the owner of the park.

**Issue:** What standard of care must landowners exercise in maintaining their property to avoid harm to all possible persons?

**Rule:** Landowners must maintain their property as a reasonable person would given the specific circumstances, including the likelihood of injury and the expense of protection against such injury. The court abandoned the distinctions between trespassers, invitees and licensees.

### Hicks v. State (1975) Ke

**Facts:** Hicks brought a wrongful death action asserting the state's negligent failure to maintain a bridge.

**Issue:** Is the state protected from negligence suits by the doctrine of "sovereign immunity?"

**Rule:** The doctrine of sovereign immunity is abolished.

### Dalehite v. United States (S.Ct. 1953) Ke

**Facts:** Dalehite was injured in an explosion at a fertilizer plant that was negligently supervised by the federal government.

**Issue:** Does the Federal Tort Claims Act allow governmental liability for negligence at the operational (but not at the planning) level?

**Rule:** (Reed, J.) The Federal Tort Claims Act allows recovery of damages caused by negligent plans, specifications or schedules of operations. Acts of subordinates in carrying out the operations of the government in accordance with official directions are not actionable.

### Pierce v. Yakima Valley Memorial Hospital Association (1953) Ke

**Facts:** The plaintiff brought a malpractice action against a charitable hospital in which the plaintiff was a paying patient.

**Issue:** Is a charitable organization immune from liability for injuries caused by the negligent conduct of its employees?

**Rule:** The doctrine of charitable immunity is abolished.

### Buch v. Amory Manufacturing Co. (1897) Ep

**Facts:** Buch, age 8, had his hand crushed by dangerous machinery while trespassing on the defendant's property. The defendant's foreman warned Buch to leave before the accident, but did not make sure that he did.

**Issue:** Does a landowner have an affirmative duty to warn an infant trespasser of dangers on the property?

**Rule:** A landowner does not have a duty to warn a trespasser of a danger, even if the trespasser is a child.

**Note:** Today, a landlord's duties to trespassers have been expanded.

### Montgomery v. National Convoy & Trucking Co. (1937) Ep

**Facts:** Montgomery's car hit the defendant's truck which, through no fault of the defendant, was stalled in the middle of the road. The defendant knew the truck was in a blind spot but did not sufficiently warn oncoming traffic.

**Issue:** Does a party have a duty to warn highway travellers of a peril it caused without negligence?

**Rule:** A party who creates a dangerous situation on a highway, even absent negligence, has a duty to other highway users to take precautions reasonably calculated to prevent injury.

### Robert Addie & Sons (Collieries), Ltd. v. Dumbreck (1928) Ep

**Facts:** The defendant did not actively protect children who frequently played on his property. The plaintiff, age 4, was killed by machinery after being warned not to play in the area.

**Issue:** Must a landowner protect an infant trespasser from hazards on the landowner's property?

**Rule:** A landowner owes no duty to a trespasser other than refraining from willful injury.

### Rowland v. Christian (1968) Ep, Fr

**Facts:** Rowland, a social guest, was injured at Christian's house by a defective faucet that Christian had known about prior to the accident.

**Issue:** Should the traditional distinctions between trespasser, invitee, and licensee be enforced?

**Rule:** An owner shall be judged by a reasonable person standard. The plaintiff's status as a trespasser, licensee, or invitee may have some bearing on the issue of liability, but is not determinative.

**Note:** This is a minority view that only a few states have adopted.

### Coggs v. Bernard (1703) Ep

**Facts:** The defendant negligently broke some bottles of brandy while he was moving them for Coggs. Although Coggs had a contract with the defendant, it was invalid because there was no consideration.

**Issue:** Is one liable for negligent performance of an unenforceable contract?

**Rule:** One who undertakes the performance of a service contract is liable for negligence in performing such service even if the contract is found to be invalid.

### Erie R.R. v. Stewart (1930) Ep

**Facts:** Stewart was injured when his truck was hit by an Erie railroad train. Erie usually maintained a watchman at the crossing, though it was not obligated to do so. Stewart relied on the presence of the watchman and interpreted the absence of warning from the watchman as an assurance of safety in crossing the tracks.

**Issue:** May one who voluntarily assumes a greater standard of care than that required by law discontinue the use of such care at any time?

**Rule:** If a party acts in accordance with a greater standard of care than that required by law, and another party relies on the provision of extra care, it may be negligent to discontinue the use of extra care without adequately warning of the discontinuance.

### Marsalis v. LaSalle (1957) Ep

**Facts:** Marsalis was scratched by LaSalle's cat. LaSalle agreed to quarantine the cat to see if it had rabies, even though he was not obligated to do so. Marsalis had to undergo painful treatments because LaSalle negligently allowed the cat to escape 5 days after the incident.

**Issue:** Is a party who promises to perform an act it is not legally obligated to perform liable for the results of improper performance.

**Rule:** Failure to reasonably perform an act that was not legally required, but was promised, gives rise to liability.

### H.R. Moch Co. v. Rensselaer Water Co. (1928) Ep

**Facts:** Rensselaer Water Co. contracted to supply water to the city. A warehouse of H.R. Moch Co. burned down because a sufficient quantity of water was not available to firefighters.

**Issue:** May a third party beneficiary of a contract bring an action in tort for nonfeasance?

**Rule:** An actor who is not a party to a contract but benefits from its performance may not recover in tort for a contracting party's nonfeasance.

### Kline v. 1500 Massachusetts Ave. Apartment Corp. (1970) Ep

**Facts:** Kline was injured when robbed in the lobby of her apartment building. The tenants had informed the defendant/landlord of previous incidents, but nothing was done.

**Issue:** Do landlords have an affirmative duty to protect their tenants from the foreseeable tortious acts of third parties?

**Rule:** Landlords must take reasonable steps to ensure the safety of their tenants from the tortious acts of third parties in areas where they have exclusive control.

### Weirum v. RKO General, Inc. (1975) Ep

**Facts:** A radio station sponsored a contest giving prizes to the first person to find its disc jockey at different locations in the city. The plaintiff was killed by a driver who was speeding to reach the disc jockey's location.

**Issue:** If one's conduct encourages a negligent response by another, is the party liable for the other's negligence?

**Rule:** If it is foreseeable that a party's conduct will cause others to behave in a negligent and dangerous manner, that party will not be relieved of liability by the intervening negligence of another.

### Tarasoff v. Regents of University of California (1976) Ep, Fr

**Facts:** Doctors at the defendant's university hospital knew that a mental patient they were releasing intended to kill Tarasoff. The defendants did not warn Tarasoff of the danger, and she was murdered.

**Issue:** Does a psychologist have a duty to warn a third party of a danger posed by one of the psychologist's patients?

**Rule:** Because of a psychologist's special relationship with a patient, the psychologist has a duty to warn third persons of the patient's violent intentions, even if the psychologist has no special relationship with the foreseeable victim.

### Farwell v. Keaton (1976) Fr

**Facts:** Farwell and Seigrist, two friends, were attacked. Seigrist attempted to treat Farwell, but after two hours left him in a car in his grandparents' driveway. Farwell died 3 days later.

**Issue:** When does a party have a duty to rescue another?

**Rule:** One who voluntarily comes to the aid of another in peril, or has a special relationship with another in peril, has a duty to rescue the party in peril if the rescue can be accomplished without risking personal danger.

### Strauss v. Belle Realty Co. (1985) Fr

**Facts:** Strauss fell down in the common area of his apartment building during a city-wide power failure.

**Issue:** Does a public utility, contracting with a landlord, owe a duty of care to the landlord's tenants?

**Rule:** A utility does not owe a duty of care to a tenant because the utility has only contracted with the landlord.

### Vince v. Wilson (1989) Fr

**Facts:** Vince was seriously injured in a car accident with Wilson's grandnephew. The plaintiff sued Wilson, who bought the car for her grandnephew, for the tort of negligent entrustment.

**Issue:** May a person who knowingly purchases a car for an incompetent driver be liable for the tort of negligent entrustment?

**Rule:** A person who knowingly purchases a car for an incompetent driver may be liable for negligent entrustment (i.e., liability from the combined negligence of both the negligence in trusting the incompetent driver with the car and the negligent operation of the car).

### Kelly v. Gwinnell (1984) Fr

**Facts:** The defendant served a number of drinks to his friend, a guest in his home, who became drunk. After his friend left the defendant's house, he was involved in a head-on collision that injured Kelly.

**Issue:** Is a host liable for the negligence of an adult social guest who has become intoxicated at the host's home?

**Rule:** A host who serves liquor to an adult social guest, knowing both that the guest is intoxicated and will thereafter be operating a motor vehicle, is liable for injuries to a third party that are a result of the guest's negligent drunk driving.

**Note:** This is the minority rule.

### Fitch v. Adler (1981) Fr

**Facts:** Fitch, a guest/licensee in Adler's home, was injured when she walked off an outside deck after Adler had opened the deck doors. Adler had failed to warn her that the deck was without guardrails. Because of darkness Fitch was unable to see this dangerous condition.
**Issue:** Does the duty of a landowner to warn a licensee of concealed dangers apply when the licensee extends beyond the area of invite?
**Rule:** When the licensee extends beyond the specified area of invite, the licensee becomes a trespasser. A landowner owes no duty to warn of concealed dangers unless this area is reasonably thought to be extended because of the landowner's direct or implied actions.

### Erickson v. Curtis Investment Co. (1989) Fr

**Facts:** The plaintiff was attacked in Curtis Investment's parking garage. An expert for the plaintiff testified that the security measures taken by Curtis Investment were inadequate under the circumstances.
**Issue:** Does the owner-operator of a commercial parking garage have a duty to protect its customers from criminal actions by third parties?
**Rule:** An owner-operator of a commercial parking garage has a duty to use reasonable care under the circumstances to deter criminal activity which may cause harm to its customers. Circumstances to be considered include the cost of security, the risk of harm which the operator knows or should know, and the location of the garage.
**Note:** This is an exception to the general business enterprise rule that a merchant-customer relationship is not enough to impose a duty on the merchant to protect its customers.

### Riss v. City of New York (1968) Fr

**Facts:** Riss was blinded and maimed by a party who had repeatedly threatened her. Her repeated requests for police protection had been denied.
**Issue:** Is a municipality liable for the negligent failure to protect a citizen from crime?
**Rule:** Local governments, through their police departments, may not be held liable in the absence of legislation for failure to protect members of the public from external hazards and the activities of criminal wrongdoers.

### Friedman v. State of New York (1986) Fr

**Facts:** Friedman's car was involved in an accident after it was sideswiped and flung into oncoming traffic. There was no road divider, though the state had previously decided that one was needed.

**Issue:** Is a state liable for failing to remedy a known dangerous situation?

**Rule:** The state may be held liable for its failure to remedy a dangerous situation of which it was aware, unless it has a legitimate state interest in doing so.

### Battalla v. State of New York (1961) Fr

**Facts:** The plaintiff suffered severe emotional and neurological distress after the defendant failed to lock a ski lift belt on him.

**Issue:** Can one recover for injuries caused by the negligent infliction of emotional harm?

**Rule:** An action may be asserted for the negligent infliction of emotional harm.

### Gammon v. Osteopathic Hospital of Maine, Inc. (1987) Fr

**Facts:** After Gammon's father died he received a bag from the Osteopathic Hospital of Maine that supposedly contained his father's personal belongings, but in fact contained a severed leg. Gammon suffered severe emotional stress, but showed no physical symptoms and sought no medical treatment.

**Issue:** Must a plaintiff show physical impact, objective manifestation, accompanying tort, or special circumstances to recover a claim for severe emotional distress without physical injury?

**Rule:** A plaintiff's claim for compensation for severe emotional distress without physical injury may not be barred solely because the plaintiff has failed to show some physical manifestation of the injury.

### Portee v. Jaffee (1980) Fr

**Facts:** The plaintiff sued for emotional distress after her son was killed when he became trapped between an elevator door and a shaft wall in Jaffee's building. The son was contributorily negligent.

**Issue:** May damages for emotional harm be reduced when the party whose injury caused the emotional harm was contributorily negligent?

**Rule:** Damages for emotional harm resulting from death or serious injury to another may be reduced if that person was contributorily negligent in causing the injury.

### Johnson v. Jamaica Hospital (1984) Fr

**Facts:** The Johnsons claimed they suffered emotional harm when their child was kidnapped from the nursery of Jamaica Hospital due to the hospital's negligence.

**Issue:** May parents recover damages for emotional harm from a hospital whose negligence caused injury to their children?

**Rule:** Parents may not recover damages from a hospital for any emotional duress suffered as a result of an injury inflicted upon their child by the hospital because the hospital does not owe a duty of care directly to the parents (only to the hospitalized children themselves).

### Burke v. Rivo (1990) Fr

**Facts:** Rivo negligently performed a sterilization operation on Burke. Burke originally chose to be sterilized for economic reasons and sued for the costs of raising the child that was conceived after the unsuccessful operation.

**Issue:** May the parents of a child conceived as a result of a physician's negligent performance of a sterilization procedure recover for the costs of rearing the child?

**Rule:** The costs of raising a child after an unsuccessful and negligently performed sterilization are reasonably foreseeable and are a natural and probable consequence of the physician's negligence. As there are no social policy concerns which require that damages be limited, the costs of raising the child are recoverable if the parents chose sterilization for economic purposes.

### Viccaro v. Milunsky (1990) Fr

**Facts:** A geneticist wrongly determined that the Viccaros could conceive children who would be free from a genetic defect that was common in the Viccaro family. A son was born to the Viccaros with the defect.

**Issue 1:** May a child born with a genetic defect sue a party whose negligence contributed to its birth?

**Rule 1:** A defendant whose negligence is a reason for a child's existence is not liable for the unfortunate consequences associated with the child's birth.

**Issue 2:** May the parents of a child born with a genetic defect recover damages from a negligent party whose negligence contributed to the child being born?

**Rule 2:** The parents of a child with a genetic birth defect may recover from the party whose negligence contributed to the child's birth, the extraordinary medical, educational, and other expenses associated with the child's disorder. They may also recover for emotional distress and any physical results thereof. However, they may not recover for the loss of companionship of a normal child, and the total damages may be offset by any benefits the parents derive from the child's existence.

# Chapter 5

## BASIC DEFENSES

I.    CONTRIBUTORY NEGLIGENCE

A plaintiff whose negligence contributed proximately to cause the injury is completely barred from recovery.

A.    Reasonable Person
A plaintiff is required to act as a reasonable person would to avoid being injured.

Exceptions:

1. Minors
A child plaintiff will be held to the standard of a reasonable child with the same age, intelligence and experience.

2. Insane Persons
The courts are split as to whether an insane person should be judged according to the reasonable person standard. Courts are more willing to use a subjective standard to judge the contributory negligence, as opposed to negligence, of an insane person since the insane person has not caused injury to another person.

B.    Unforeseeable Manner
If one's negligence creates a risk to oneself of a particular harm being brought about in a particular manner, the person is not contributorily negligent if the harm occurs in an unforeseeable manner.

Example:
Rob warns Susan not to go in his room because she might cut herself on a broken window pane. Susan enters the room and is cut by a knife which was left on the floor. Although the cut she received was the same injury that was risked by her entry, she was not contributorily negligent because the harm was brought

about in an unforeseeable manner, from the knife as opposed to the broken window pane.

C.    Affirmative Defense
A defendant must specifically plead and prove a plaintiff's contributory negligence.

D.    Perilous Situation
Remaining in a perilous situation may constitute contributory negligence.

E.    Applicability
Contributory negligence does not apply to strict liability, intentional torts, or negligence per se.

F.    Contributory Negligence v. Failure to Mitigate
Generally, if one fails to mitigate damages after the accident has occurred, it is not contributory negligence. Usually, contributory negligence occurs before the accident, while the failure to mitigate damages occurs after the accident.

Exception:
A plaintiff's failure to wear a seat belt while driving is not usually construed as contributory negligence, but rather as a failure to mitigate. Thus, damages will be lowered as opposed to barred.

II.    LAST CLEAR CHANCE

A.    Generally
This defense is actually a response to a defendant's claim that the plaintiff was contributorily negligent. If the plaintiff was contributorily negligent, but can show that the defendant still had the last clear chance to avoid causing the accident, then the plaintiff is not barred from recovering damages.

B.    Applicability
The last clear chance doctrine applies whenever the defendant is aware of the plaintiff's danger and does not alleviate it,

regardless of whether the plaintiff was helpless to avoid the danger or was inattentive to a means of avoiding the danger. If, however, the defendant did not know of the plaintiff's danger but should have, the last clear chance doctrine only applies if the plaintiff was helpless, as opposed to inattentive.

|  | **Inattentive Defendant** | **Aware Defendant** |
|---|---|---|
| **Helpless Plaintiff** | Last clear chance applies (Plaintiff recovers) | Last clear chance applies (Plaintiff recovers) |
| **Inattentive Plaintiff** | Last clear chance does not apply (Plaintiff does not recover) | Last clear chance applies (Plaintiff recovers) |

## III. COMPARATIVE NEGLIGENCE

A. Generally

This doctrine was developed in reaction to the all or nothing approach of contributory negligence. It rejects the all or nothing result and instead divides liability between the plaintiff and the defendant based on their relative degrees of fault.

There are two basic types of comparative negligence:

1. Pure Form — Minority View

A plaintiff can recover for damages caused by a defendant even if the plaintiff was more at fault in causing the accident.

Example:

Rob, a plaintiff, is 70% responsible for causing an accident; Susan, the defendant, is 30% responsible. Susan has to pay Rob 30% of the total damages.

2. Modified 50% Rule — Majority View
Only a plaintiff who is equally or less negligent than a defendant can recover, i.e., as long as the plaintiff is not more than 50% liable for causing the accident, the defendant has to pay a share of damages. But, if the plaintiff is 51% responsible, then the defendant has no liability.

B. Policy Behind Comparative Negligence

1. The tort system is based on fault and the extent of each party's fault should govern the extent of its liability. Thus, a plaintiff should be allowed to recover damages even if there was contributory negligence.

2. Defendants have more of an incentive to be careful under a system of comparative negligence, as opposed to a system of contributory negligence, since a plaintiff's negligence does not bar recovery.

C. Apportionment of Liability
Usually, the percentage of fault assigned to the plaintiff is determined by examining the relative degree to which the plaintiff's conduct deviated from the standard of reasonableness, as opposed to how much it actually contributed to the accident.

IV. ASSUMPTION OF RISK

A. Generally
If the plaintiff had knowledge of and voluntarily assumed an unreasonable risk that the defendant created, the plaintiff is barred from any recovery.

There are two types of assumption of risk:

1. Express Assumption of Risk
The plaintiff may explicitly agree with the defendant, in advance of being injured, not to hold the defendant liable for any injuries. Express agreements will be enforced unless they are contrary to public policy.

Public policy issues to consider:

a. The relative bargaining power of the plaintiff and the defendant.

b. Whether the waiver of liability was apparent to the plaintiff, or would have been apparent to a reasonable person.

c. The scope of the waiver, e.g., a waiver of liability for negligence will not waive liability for grossly negligent or intentionally tortious conduct.

2. Implied Assumption of Risk

Even in the absence of an express agreement, a plaintiff can still assume the risk if:

a. the plaintiff knows of the risk, and

b. the plaintiff's actions imply a voluntary assumption of the risk.

Examples:

a. Spectators are held to impliedly assume certain risks when they go to a sporting event and are injured as a natural and foreseeable result of the sport.

b. Firefighters and police officers cannot sue for injuries sustained in their lines of work since they knowingly and voluntarily undertake the risk.

B.   Limitation on Assumption of Risk

1. Some courts treat assumption of the risk as a form of contributory negligence such that it is not a defense if the assumption of the risk was reasonable, i.e., not negligent.

2. In states that have adopted the comparative negligence doctrine, assumption of risk is not an absolute bar to recovery, but rather only a consideration to be taken into account when determining the plaintiff's degree of fault.

## V.    STATUTES OF LIMITATIONS

Broadly speaking, a statute of limitations puts a limit on the amount of time a plaintiff has to bring a lawsuit. They usually run from the time the plaintiff is injured.

An issue arises as to when the statute of limitations should begin in negligence actions where the plaintiff is injured but does not discover the injury until after the statute would have expired:

A.    Traditional View
The statute begins to run at the time of the defendant's negligent act. The time of discovery of injury is irrelevant.

B.    Modern Views (Malpractice)

1. Statute begins to run after the injury is discovered or would have been discovered by a reasonable person.

2. Statute begins to run after the physician-patient relationship is terminated.

3. Statute begins to run when the injury is discovered only in cases where a foreign object was left in the patient's body after surgery.

4. Statute begins to run after the injury and its possible cause is discovered.

## VI.   IMMUNITY

An immunity is a defense to liability in tort that is given to members of a protected class. The granting of immunity to a class of persons is based on their status or special relationship to the plaintiff.

A. Family Immunity
At common law there are two types of familial tort immunity: parent-child and husband-wife. The immunity granted is for personal injuries only.

1. Reasons for Granting Familial Immunity

   Mnemonic: **CLOT**

   a. Fear of **C**ollusion between family members,

   b. Fear of **L**itigation involving trivial disputes that would clog up the courts,

   c. **O**neness of husband and wife,

   d. To encourage peace and **T**ranquility within the family.

2. Exceptions

   a. The husband-wife immunity has been abolished or severely limited in a majority of states. The parent-child immunity has been abolished in about one-third of the states.

   b. There is no familial immunity for intentional torts.

   c. Spousal immunity does not apply to a tort that occurred before the marriage or to a suit commenced after the marriage is dissolved.

   d. Spousal immunity does not bar one from suing a party that is vicariously liable for a spouse's torts.

e. Parent-child immunity does not apply if the child is an adult, the parent is a step-parent, or one party dies before the suit is begun.

3. Reasonable Parent Standard
In states where parents have no tort immunity against their children, the parents' duty of care to the children is that of a reasonable parent. Courts will consider such factors as the child's age, physical health and intelligence, the number of children in the family, and the circumstances of the accident.

B. Charitable Immunity
At common law, charitable institutions were granted immunity from tort actions. Today, charitable immunity has either been abolished or severely limited.

1. Liability Insurance
The principle reason for abolishing this immunity is the widespread availability of liability insurance.

2. Limitations
In states that still maintain an immunity for charitable organizations, the following limitations are used:

a. Some have abolished it as to hospitals, but allow it for religious or other charitable organizations.

b. Some have allowed it to apply only if the plaintiff was a beneficiary of the charity.

C. Governmental Immunity

1. Federal Government
At common law, "the King could do no wrong" and was immune from all tort actions unless he consented to being sued. This rule was initially adopted in America. However, in 1946, with the passage of the Federal Tort Claims Act, the federal government waived its immunity in cases of ". . . injury or loss of property or personal injury or death caused

by the negligent or wrongful act or omission of any employee of the Government while acting within the scope of his office or employment" if the claim was of a nature that the United States would be liable if it were a private person.

Exceptions:

a. Intentional Torts
There is still immunity for intentional torts, except for assault, battery, false imprisonment or arrest, abuse of process and malicious prosecution committed by investigative or law enforcement officers.

b. Discretionary Acts
There is still immunity for decisions made at the planning level, as distinguished from ministerial acts at operational level. For example, if a government agency negligently harms a plaintiff because of improper agency procedures, there is no liability because the procedures are formulated at the planning level.

2. State Government
The traditional state government immunity is gradually disappearing. The main reasons for this change is the availability of liability insurance and the inappropriateness today of the idea that "the King can do no wrong."

a. In states that have not abolished immunity, it extends to state agencies such as jails, social services and health agencies.

b. States that have abolished a general governmental immunity still retain immunity for state courts and legislatures.

3. Local Governments
Traditionally, local governments have had at least a limited immunity protecting them from liability arising out of governmental as opposed to proprietary functions. However,

because of the difficulty in distinguishing between these functions, many courts have abolished the immunity either completely or at least in cases where the city/local government is insured against liability.

a. Governmental Functions
Usually involve police and fire departments, health, education and other functions traditionally carried out by the government.

b. Proprietary Functions
Functions that tend to produce revenues, such as utilities or airports. Generally, these are functions that could be performed by the private sector.

c. Standard of Care
Where local governments do not have any immunity at all, the standard of care that is applicable to them is lower than that used generally in tort.

4. Public Officials
Apart from the immunity conferred on governments, a public official who is acting within the scope of official duties is privileged against tort actions for any damages that result from discretionary conduct.

Judges, legislators and senior administrative officials have a broader immunity than other public officials. Judges and legislators, acting within the scope of their duties, are not liable even if they acted maliciously or to further their own interests. Senior officials lose their immunity if they act in bad faith.

## CASE CLIPS

### Butterfield v. Forrester (1809) Ke, Ep

**Facts:** The plaintiff was thrown from his horse when the horse hit a pole left in the road by the defendant. The plaintiff was riding very fast and evidence suggested that the pole could have been seen from 100 yards away.

**Issue:** May a defendant's negligence be excused by a plaintiff's failure to exercise ordinary care?

**Rule:** A plaintiff is barred from recovering damages caused by another's negligence when the exercise of ordinary care by the plaintiff could have prevented the accident.

### Clark v. Boston & Maine Railroad (1935) Ke

**Facts:** Clark was injured when he stood on the defendant's railroad tracks with his back to an oncoming train.

**Issue:** Is a contributorily negligent plaintiff necessarily barred from recovering against a negligent defendant?

**Rule:** Under the "last clear chance" doctrine a negligent plaintiff may recover from a subsequently negligent defendant who could have avoided the accident. The plaintiff has the burden of proving that the defendant had the last clear chance to avoid the accident.

### LeRoy Fibre Co. v. Chicago, Milwaukee & St. Paul Ry. (S.Ct. 1914) Ke, Ep

**Facts:** LeRoy Fibre Co. asserted an action for the value of flax burned when a spark flew out of the defendant's negligently operated locomotive. The railroad company claimed that the storage of the flax on the plaintiff's property next to the tracks was contributorily negligent.

**Issue:** May the use of one's property be limited by the chance that a neighbor may be negligent?

**Rule:** (McKenna, J.) The right to use one's own property cannot be limited by the wrongs of another.

### Spier v. Barker (1974) Ke

**Facts:** Spier suffered extensive injuries because she was not wearing a seat belt when Barker's truck negligently hit her car.

**Issue:** May damages be reduced for a plaintiff who failed to use a seat belt?

**Rule:** If a plaintiff failed to mitigate damages by wearing a seat belt, damages should be apportioned such that the defendant is only liable for those that would have occurred had the plaintiff been wearing a seat belt.

### Li v. Yellow Cab Co. of California (1975) Ke, Ep

**Facts:** Li negligently made a left-hand turn at an intersection, hitting a driver for Yellow Cab who was speeding through a yellow traffic light.

**Issue:** Is a contributorily negligent plaintiff completely barred from recovery?

**Rule:** When both parties have been negligent, liability shall be apportioned according to their relative degrees of fault. (Pure comparative negligence.)

**Note:** There is no need for the last clear chance doctrine under a system of pure comparative negligence.

### Lovell v. Oahe Electric Cooperative (1986) Ke

**Facts:** Lovell was awarded damages under the state's comparative negligence statute, which allowed a plaintiff who was only slightly negligent to recover damages reduced in proportion to the amount of the plaintiff's contributory negligence.

**Issue:** Must a judge direct a verdict for a defendant when a plaintiff's negligence was greater than the defendant's?

**Rule:** When the facts show beyond a reasonable doubt that a plaintiff's negligence was greater than the defendant's, it is the function of the court to find in favor of the defendant.

### Farwell v. The Boston and Worcester Rail Road Corp. (1842) Ke

**Facts:** Farwell, the defendant's employee, was injured when the defendant's train derailed due to another employee's negligence.

**Issue:** Does one assume the risks inherent in one's employment?

**Rule:** A party who is employed for compensation takes upon himself the natural risks and perils incident to the performance of his job.

**Note:** Today it is unlikely that a court would allow this result, because of a general policy against the "contracting away" of liability.

### Lamson v. American Axe & Tool Co. (1900) Ke, Ep

**Facts:** Lamson, a hatchet painter, complained that the racks on which the hatchets were hung to dry were dangerous. He was told to use the racks or lose his job. Lamson was injured by a falling hatchet.

**Issue:** Does an employee impliedly assume a risk when the employee continues working, fully aware of a potential danger of the job?

**Rule:** An employee has assumed the risk and may not recover for an injury if the employee continues working despite the employer's refusal to correct a potential hazard identified by the employee.

### Paubel v. Hitz (1936) Ke

**Facts:** The plaintiff slipped on the sidewalk outside the defendant's place of business. Both parties knew that the sidewalk was slippery.

**Issue:** Are landowners required to warn an invitee of conditions which are obvious and known to the invitee?

**Rule:** Landowners owe an invitee a duty to maintain their premises so they are reasonably safe and to warn of unsafe conditions only if they are neither obvious nor known to the invitee.

### Clayards v. Dethick (1848) Ke

**Facts:** The plaintiff's horse died when it fell in a ditch dug by the defendant. The plaintiff knew of the ditch because he had passed it earlier in the day and was warned by the defendant's employees.

**Issue:** Has one assumed the risk of another's negligence when one proceeds despite warnings of the risk?

**Rule:** One does not assume the risk of another's negligence by proceeding despite knowledge of the risk, unless the danger was so great that no sensible person would have incurred it.

### Jefferson County Bank of Lakewood v. Armored Motors Service (1961) Ke

**Facts:** Jefferson County Bank sued Armored Motors Service after the money they were transporting was stolen. Though both parties agreed by contract to limit the defendant's liability, Jefferson sued for an amount in excess of the agreed upon amount.

**Issue:** Can one limit liability for negligence through contract?

**Rule:** Liability for the negligent acts of a bailee can be contractually limited if both parties have a thorough understanding of the contract's provisions and equal bargaining power.

### Siragusa v. Swedish Hospital (1962) Ke

**Facts:**  Siragusa was injured at work by a metal hook on a door.

**Issue:**  Does an employee "assume the risk" of an unsafe work area by staying on the job?

**Rule:**  An employer who negligently fails to provide employees with reasonably safe working conditions cannot assert the defense of "assumption of the risk."

### McConville v. State Farm Mutual
### Automobile Insurance Co. (1962) Ke

**Facts:**  The plaintiff, a passenger in the defendant's car, sued the defendant and her insurer for injuries sustained in a car accident.

**Issue:**  Does a guest/passenger assume the risk of negligence by the host/driver?

**Rule:**  The driver of an automobile owes a guest the same duty of care as to other persons. The guest is not implied to have assumed the risk of negligent driving.

### Salinas v. Vierstra (1985) Ke

**Facts:**  Salinas lost his tort action when a jury accepted his employer's defense that Salinas had assumed the risk inherent in his employment. This defense conflicted with the state's comparative negligence laws.

**Issue:**  Is the doctrine of assumption of risk still valid?

**Rule:**  Except where an individual expressly consents to contractually assume the risk involved, the assumption of risk defense no longer has any legal effect. Issues of nonexpress assumption of risk are decided by using principles of comparative negligence.

### Tunkl v. Regents of the University of California (1963) Ke

**Facts:**  Tunkl signed a form releasing a charitable hospital from any liability for negligent acts. This was a condition of admission.

**Issue:**  Is an agreement to relieve a hospital of liability for negligent acts valid?

**Rule:**  Public interest will void an agreement limiting a hospital's liability for negligence.

### Beems v. Chicago, Rock Island & Peoria R.R. Co. (1882) Ep

**Fact:**  Beems died while trying to uncouple two railroad cars of a moving train. Beems had signalled the other workers to slow down the train, but they failed to do so. The court rejected the defendants' argument that Beems was contributorily negligent.

**Issue:** What is the effect of a court's rejection of a contributory negligence defense?

**Rule:** A negligent defendant will be completely liable if the plaintiff is found to be free of contributory negligence.

### Gyerman v. United States Lines Co. (1972) Ep

**Facts:** Gyerman, a longshoreman, was injured while unloading sacks that he knew were stacked dangerously.

**Issue:** Which party has the burden of proving the elements of contributory negligence?

**Rule:** The defendant has the burden of proving that the plaintiff's own negligence contributed to the injury.

### Derheim v. N. Fiorito Co. (1972) Ep

**Facts:** The plaintiff was not wearing his seat belt when he was injured in a collision caused by the defendant's negligence.

**Issue:** Is the failure to wear a seat belt contributory negligence?

**Rule:** Failure to use a seat belt is not contributory negligence because it is not the cause of an accident.

### Kumkumian v. City of New York (1953) Ep

**Facts:** Kumkumian was found dead under a subway car that had made an emergency stop after the engineer had twice attempted to drive over the track, but was unable to because of the plaintiff's body on the tracks. These attempts to drive on probably killed the plaintiff.

**Issue:** May a negligent plaintiff recover damages against a negligent defendant when the defendant had a chance to avoid the accident?

**Rule:** Under the last clear chance doctrine, a plaintiff's negligence is not the proximate cause of the plaintiff's injury when a negligent defendant had the last clear chance to avoid the accident.

### Murphy v. Steeplechase Amusement Co. (1929) Ep, Fr

**Facts:** Murphy fell while riding an amusement park ride that dropped people onto cushions.

**Issue:** May one recover for an injury received from a perceived risk?

**Rule:** One who takes part in a sport accepts its inherent, obvious and necessary dangers.

### Meistrich v. Casino Arena Attractions, Inc. (1959) Ep

**Facts:** Meistrich continued to skate on the defendant's ice rink after noticing that its corners were too slippery for ordinary skaters.

**Issue:** Are assumption of risk and contributory negligence distinct and independent defenses?

**Rule:** Assumption of risk is not a separate defense from contributory negligence. If a plaintiff impliedly assumes a risk, the plaintiff is considered to be contributorily negligent.

### Obstetrics & Gynecologists v. Pepper (1985) Ep

**Facts:** Treatment at a medical clinic was conditioned on the signing of an irrevocable arbitration agreement expressly waiving the right to a trial. Pepper was injured by a drug prescribed by the medical clinic. She did not recall signing the agreement or having it explained by an employee of the medical clinic.

**Issue:** Is an arbitration clause of an adhesion contract enforceable against the adhering party?

**Rule:** Though an adhesion contract is enforceable if it falls within the reasonable expectations of the weaker party and is not unduly oppressive, courts will not enforce a contractual provision limiting the duties or liabilities of a stronger party absent plain and clear notification of the terms of the contract and an understanding consent to such terms by the weaker party.

### American Motorcycle Association v. Superior Court (1978) Ep

**Facts:** The plaintiff was injured in a motorcycle race for novices which was negligently organized by the defendants, the American Motorcycle Association. The defendants filed a crossclaim against the plaintiff's parents for their negligent supervision of their child.

**Issue:** Can the indemnity doctrine be modified to allow only partial, proportional indemnity among concurrent tortfeasors?

**Rule:** Under the doctrine of partial equitable indemnity, the apportionment of loss among codefendants on pure comparative principles is permitted.

### Berkovitz by Berkovitz v. United States (S.Ct. 1988) Ep

**Facts:** Berkovitz was injured by a dose of a contaminated polio vaccine. the defendants, having approved the production and release of that vaccine, asserted the "discretionary function" exception.

**Issue:** When may government officials invoke the discretionary function exception to avoid liability for decisions which involve the permissible exercise of policy judgment?
**Rule:** (Marshall, J.) The discretionary function exception will be barred as a defense to liability only where the organization's policy leaves no room for an official to exercise discretion, or if the act does not involve the exercise of discretion.

### Harlow v. Fitzgerald (S.Ct. 1982) Ep
**Facts:** The defendants, aides to President Nixon, were instrumental in influencing the President to fire Harlow, an Air Force employee who had testified about huge cost overruns in the Air Force.
**Issue:** Are senior aides and advisors to the President of the United States entitled to immunity for damages caused by official acts?
**Rule:** (Powell, J.) Presidential aides are not immune for official acts if they knew or reasonably should have known that the actions they took within their sphere of official responsibility violated the constitutional rights of the plaintiff, or if they maliciously intended to deprive the plaintiff of constitutional rights.

### Brown v. San Francisco Ball Club, Inc. (1950) Fr
**Facts:** Brown was struck by a wildly thrown baseball while she was sitting in the stands behind first base.
**Issue:** Are the dangers inherent in attending a baseball game so obvious that a spectator impliedly "assumes the risk?"
**Rule:** By voluntarily entering into a baseball stadium as a spectator, one accepts the reasonable risks and hazards inherent and incidental to the sport.

### Verduce v. Board of Higher Education (1959) Fr
**Facts:** Verduce fell down a staircase when she exited the stage without looking down during an opera rehearsal. The director had told her not to look down when exiting or she would be fired.
**Issue:** Can one recover for injuries resulting from a known danger?
**Rule:** A person must exercise reasonable care in regard to one's own safety. Ignoring a known danger for personal motives is no excuse.

### Santangelo v. State of New York (1988) Fr

**Facts:** The plaintiffs, police officers, were injured while capturing a mental patient who was negligently allowed to escape from a state hospital.

**Issue:** May a police officer injured in the line of duty sue a party who negligently created the need for their services?

**Rule:** Because it is the duty of the police to deal on behalf of the public with emergencies created by negligence, they may not sue a party who has negligently created the need for their services.

**Note:** Firefighters may not sue those who negligently caused a fire.

### Gonzalez v. Garcia (1977) Fr

**Facts:** The plaintiff was injured while he was a passenger in a car driven by a driver he knew to be intoxicated.

**Issue:** What effect does the adoption of comparative negligence have upon the defense of implied assumption of the risk?

**Rule:** Adoption of a comparative negligence standard results in the merger of implied assumption of risk and comparative negligence. Express assumption of risk still remains as a separate defense.

### Albritton v. Neighborhood Centers Association
### For Child Development (1984) Fr

**Facts:** Albritton's daughter was allegedly injured at the defendant's day care center. The defendant was a nonprofit corporation.

**Issue:** Is the doctrine of charitable immunity valid in Ohio?

**Rule:** There is no immunity for charitable organizations in Ohio. Allowing immunity forces injured parties to make a contribution to the charity which caused the injury and often results in other governmental assistance agencies and other charities bearing the burden of the loss. Further, the fear that charitable organizations will cease to exist if immunity is abolished is unfounded.

### Winn v. Gilroy (1984) Fr

**Facts:** The plaintiff sued her husband after her two children were killed in a car accident caused by her husband's drunk driving.

**Issue:** May a parent be liable to a child for injuries caused?

**Rule:** Although general familial tort immunity has been abolished, parents still retain some privilege due to the special relationship they have with their children. However, where parents have failed to fulfill the general duty of ordinary care to avoid foreseeable injury, they may be liable.

# Chapter 6

## CAUSATION OF HARM

I.   SINE QUA NON ("BUT FOR" CAUSATION)

The basic test to determine if there was causation in fact is to ask whether "but for" a defendant's negligence a plaintiff's injuries would have resulted.

This test is too broad, however, because it does not bar liability for the remote results of one's conduct.

The test is also underinclusive because it does not allow recovery in cases of joint causation since "but for" one cause the other cause would have hurt the plaintiff anyway.

II.  PROOF OF CAUSATION

One does not have to prove that "but for" a defendant's negligence the injury would not have occurred. It is sufficient to prove by a preponderance of the evidence that the defendant's negligence increased the risk that the accident would occur.

III. CONCURRENT CAUSES

If one's injury is caused by the combined negligence of multiple tortfeasors, liability will be determined according to one of several tests.

A.   Substantial Factor Test
In cases where the negligent actions of each tortfeasor alone would have caused the entire injury by itself and the harm is indivisible such that damages cannot be apportioned among the tortfeasors, each is liable for causing the entire harm. To be liable, a defendant's negligence must have played a substantial part in causing the harm.

B.    Multiple Negligence
In cases where the negligent actions of each defendant would not have caused the injury alone, each is liable for the damage each defendant actually caused.

C.    Alternative Causes
If it cannot be determined which of the two negligent actors caused the injury, both are liable unless one can prove his innocence.

D.    Enterprise Liability Theory
Each member of an enterprise is liable for damages caused by the enterprise as a whole when there has been close cooperation among the different members and damages cannot be apportioned.

IV.    LIABILITY AND JOINDER OF DEFENDANTS

A.    Plaintiff Recovers Once
A plaintiff can only recover once for an injury, i.e., the entire amount paid by all the joint tortfeasors has to equal the value of the plaintiff's damages.

B.    Indivisible Harm
If more than one tortfeasor was a proximate cause of an injury and the harm to a plaintiff is indivisible, then each tortfeasor is liable for the entire harm, i.e., jointly and severally liable. If one party does not pay its share of the damages, the other parties will have to pay for that share.

1. Burden of Proof
The defendants have the burden of proving apportionment of the harm among themselves. Harm that occurs from successive accidents is sometimes considered indivisible.

2. Those To Whom Joint and Several Liability Applies

    a. Concurrent Tortfeasors
    Each defendant acts independently of the others, but they all combine to cause a single indivisible injury.

    b. Joint Tortfeasors
    All the defendants have acted together to harm the plaintiff.

C.    Divisible Harm
If the harm is divisible then each tortfeasor is only liable for that part of the harm that each proximately caused, unless the two tortfeasors acted in concert. If one party does not pay its share, the other parties are still only liable for their own shares.

## V.    SATISFACTION AND RELEASE

A.    Satisfaction
Once a party has recovered the entire value of its injury from the defendant(s), the party may no longer collect against the other defendant(s).

B.    Release
If a party settles its case with one of the defendants, this may release the other defendants from liability unless the party manifests an intent to still hold the other defendants liable.

## VI.    CONTRIBUTION

This is an action by one party against the other jointly and severally liable parties in order to recover the amount the party had to pay in excess of its share of the damages.

A.    Not Applicable to:

     1. Intentional Tortfeasors

     2. Worker's Compensation Cases

     3. Individual Defense
     For example, a party who has some defense that makes it not liable to the original plaintiff, even though it acted in concert with the other parties.

B.    Settlement
If one party settles with a plaintiff, it is entitled to contribution from its cotortfeasors if the settlement amount was reasonable. The settling party may nevertheless have to pay contribution to other parties who go to court and lose their cases. Some courts, in the latter case, reduce the plaintiff's total claim by the amount of the first party's pro rata share, so that the other parties cannot get contribution.

## VII. INDEMNITY

Indemnity is the shifting of the entire loss to the tortfeasor with a disproportionate share of the culpability. Unlike contribution, the court makes a 100% shift in payment.

Examples:

A.    Passive Negligence
A passively negligent defendant can recover from one who is actively negligent.

B.    Reliance
A retailer who relies on the quality control of a manufacturer may recover from the manufacturer if a defective product causes damage.

C.   Degree
In situations where there are vast differences in the degrees of fault of each defendant, one defendant may have to take the responsibility for all the damages.

D.   Vicariously Liable
One defendant may be vicariously liable for another's negligence due to a legal relationship (e.g., employer-employee).

## CASE CLIPS

### Barnes v. Bovenmyer (1963) Ke
**Facts:** The plaintiff lost his eye because the defendant, his doctor, failed to find a piece of steel that was in the eye upon examination.
**Issue:** Is an actor liable for a negligent act when it is less than likely that the resulting injury was caused by it?
**Rule:** A party may not recover for the negligence of another unless "but for" the negligence, the injury would not have resulted.

### Waffen v. United States Dept. of Health & Human Services (1986) Ke
**Facts:** Waffen's cancer was negligently diagnosed. Consequently, a delay in treatment ensued during which the cancer became terminal.
**Issue:** What burden of proof must plaintiffs satisfy to successfully claim that a defendant's negligence deprived them of a substantial possibility of survival?
**Rule:** Plaintiffs must prove by a "preponderance of the evidence" that a defendant's negligence actually deprived them of a substantial possibility of survival.

### Kingston v. Chicago & Northwestern Railway (1927) Ke, Ep
**Facts:** Two separate fires, one started by defendant's negligence and one of unknown origin, destroyed Kingston's property.
**Issue:** When the defendant's negligence combines with a cause of unknown origin, which party bears the burden of proof to determine if the unknown condition was of innocent origin?

**Rule:** Under the concurrent liability rule, when two conditions jointly cause harm, a negligent defendant will be liable for damages unless the defendant can prove the other condition was of innocent origin.

### Allen v. United States (1984) Ke

**Facts:** The plaintiffs sued the United States claiming that their illnesses were caused by the government's testing of the atom bomb.
**Issue:** Must a plaintiff show the precise connection between a defendant's act and the plaintiff's injury to establish cause-in-fact?
**Rule:** When a defendant negligently creates a hazard that puts an identifiable population group at increased risk, a member of that group that develops a condition which is consistent with the hazard need only show that the defendant's conduct was more likely than not a substantial factor contributing to the plaintiff's injury.

### Johnson v. Chapman (1897) Ke

**Facts:** The defendants were negligent in maintaining a wall common to both their warehouses. The wall collapsed, injuring the plaintiff.
**Issue:** Can two defendants be held jointly liable when their separate negligent acts caused an injury?
**Rule:** Two persons separately and independently contributing to an injury may be held jointly and severally liable for the entire injury. A court will hold each proportionally liable.

### Knell v. Feltman (1949) Ke

**Facts:** Feltman and Knell were involved in a car accident in which Knell's passenger was injured. Both were negligently responsible, but the passenger only sued Feltman, who brought a third-party complaint against Knell to have the court force Knell to share in the damages.
**Issue:** Is contribution between two concurrently negligent tortfeasors allowed when only one was named in a plaintiff's action?
**Rule:** The right to seek contribution belongs to tortfeasors who must pay damages and it permits the inclusion of concurrently negligent tortfeasors, even if there was not a joint judgment against them.

### Hillman v. Wallin (1974) Ke

**Facts:** Hillman was hit in the eye with a plastic hose that several boys were playing with while riding in a school bus. Wallin, the bus driver, was aware that the boys were playing with the hose, but he did not stop them.

**Issue:** Can a defendant who is passively negligent seek indemnity from defendants who are actively negligent?

**Rule:** A party who is passively negligent in failing to supervise actively negligent persons is only secondarily liable and can recover indemnification from the actively negligent defendants.

### Tolbert v. Gerber Industries, Inc. (1977) Ke

**Facts:** Defendants, a manufacturer and an installer of defective equipment, were found jointly and severally liable. The trial court ordered 100% indemnity for the installer from the manufacturer.

**Issue:** May a joint tortfeasor, who was "passively" or "secondarily" negligent seek full indemnification from the other tortfeasor, who was "actively" or "primarily" negligent, or should the joint tortfeasors be liable according to their degrees of culpability?

**Rule:** Each joint tortfeasor should pay their proportional share of the negligence since indemnity is not available to one joint tortfeasor who was passively negligent in discovering the other's negligence.

### New York Central R.R. v. Grimstad (1920) Ep

**Facts:** Grimstad, who could not swim, fell off the defendant's boat. Although the boat was not equipped with life preservers, the defendant claimed that Grimstad would have drowned even if he had a life preserver.

**Issue:** May a negligent party be liable for an injury even though the injury would have occurred regardless of the negligence?

**Rule:** A defendant who has been negligent will not be liable for damages when "but for" the defendant's conduct, the injury would have occurred anyway.

### Stimpson v. Wellington Service Corp. (1969) Ep

**Facts:** The plaintiff claimed that the pipes in his basement became uncoupled because the defendants drove their 137-ton rig in violation of a statutory weight limitation.

**Issue:** Must a plaintiff exclude other possible causes to establish that a defendant's negligence was the cause in fact of the damages?

**Rule:** A plaintiff is not required to exclude other possible causes. It is sufficient for the plaintiff to show that the defendant's negligent act was the probable cause in fact of the damages.

### Richardson v. Richardson-Merrell (1986) Ep

**Facts:** Richardson alleged that her child's severe limb deformities were caused by a drug she took during pregnancy, which was manufactured by Richardson-Merrell.

**Issue:** Is circumstantial evidence sufficient to show that a drug is the cause in fact of an injury?

**Rule:** A plaintiff has the burden of proving, by a preponderance of the evidence, that a drug in question can cause injury and that the drug was the cause of the plaintiff's injury. Evidence must be given on which a reasonable jury could conclude that the injury was more likely than not caused by the drug.

### Herskovits v. Group Health Cooperative of Puget Sound (1983) Ep

**Facts:** The defendant failed to diagnose Herskovits' lung cancer, thereby reducing his chances for survival. The defendant argued Herskovits would have died anyway so it was not the cause in fact of his death.

**Issue:** Are defendants liable when, by their negligence, they increase the risk of harm to one who might have suffered the harm anyway?

**Rule:** If a defendant's acts or omissions increase a pre-existing risk of harm to another the defendant is only liable for a proportionate share of the harm caused.

### City of Piqua v. Morris (1918) Ep

**Facts:** The City of Piqua maintained a series of overflow ducts to its ponds that were negligently allowed to clog up. During a severe storm, water overflowed from the ducts and flooded the plaintiff's property. The flooding would have occurred regardless of the negligence.

**Issue:** Is a negligent party responsible for damages not caused by the party's negligence?

**Rule:** A party is not liable when "but for" the negligent act, the damages would have occurred anyway.

### Summers v. Tice (1948) Ep, Fr

**Facts:** A bullet struck Summers when the two defendant's negligently fired their rifles. It was unknown which gun fired the bullet.

**Issue:** Can two negligent actors be held jointly liable for an injury that only one of them could have caused?

**Rule:** Two negligent parties who act in concert are jointly liable for an injury only one of them could have committed, unless they are able to prove which one of them committed the act that caused the injury.

### Sindell v. Abbott Laboratories (1980) Ep

**Facts:** Sindell alleged that she suffered injuries from a drug manufactured by the defendants and approximately 195 other companies.

**Issue:** When several manufacturers distribute the same product, how should liability for damages caused by the product be apportioned?

**Rule:** When several manufacturers produce identical products which injure a plaintiff, and it is impossible to know which manufacturer produced the specific product that caused the injury, the liability of the defendants is proportionate to their share of the overall market. To avoid such liability, a manufacturer would have to prove its product did not cause plaintiff's injuries.

### Stubbs v. City of Rochester (1919) Fr

**Facts:** The plaintiff became infected with typhoid after drinking water supplied by the defendants. Evidence indicated that drinking water and firefighting water had been negligently mixed.

**Issue:** Must a plaintiff prove that no possible cause other than the defendant's negligence caused the plaintiff's injury?

**Rule:** The mere possibility that the cause in fact of a plaintiff's injury was not the defendant's negligence does not obligate the plaintiff to disprove the applicability of all possible causes.

### Falcon v. Memorial Hospital (1990) Fr

**Facts:** Falcon suffered from a respiratory and cardiac collapse and died after giving birth. Had her physicians inserted an intravenous line, she would have had a 37.5% greater chance of surviving.

**Issue:** May a person recover for a lost opportunity of avoiding physical harm which is less that 50%?

**Rule:** A person may recover for any *substantial* loss of opportunity of avoiding physical harm. However, one may only recover an amount equal to the percent chance lost times the value of the total harm incurred.

**Note:**   A 37.5% greater chance of survival was considered substantial.

### Mauro v. Raymark Industries, Inc. (1989) Fr

**Facts:**   Mauro was exposed to asbestos and sued for the enhanced risk of developing cancer. The experts he presented at trial could not quantify the risk he faced of developing the disease.

**Issue:**   May one recover from a private entity for an unquantified enhanced risk of disease resulting from exposure to toxic chemicals?

**Rule:**   One may not recover from a private entity for an unquantified enhanced risk of disease resulting from the exposure to toxic chemicals, unless its occurrence is established as a matter of reasonable medical probability.

### Hymowitz v. Eli Lilly & Co. (1989) Fr

**Facts:**   The plaintiffs alleged that they were injured by prenatal exposure to the drug DES. There were approximately 300 manufacturers who at one time produced DES, and there were numerous DES cases pending. DES had a single chemical composition and was marketed generically.

**Issue:**   May a plaintiff recover against the manufacturer of a generically marketed drug when identification of the producer of the specific drug that caused the plaintiff's injury is impossible?

**Rule:**   When there are numerous plaintiffs and numerous defendant manufacturers, and neither the plaintiffs nor the defendants can identify who caused each plaintiff's injuries, plaintiffs may recover from each defendant an amount of damages which corresponds to the defendant's share of the national market.

**Note:**   Defendants who can prove that their drug did not injure a particular plaintiff are not relieved of liability since liability is no longer based on the causal link between a particular defendant and a particular plaintiff, but rather is based on each defendant's overall liability.

# Chapter 7

## PROXIMATE CAUSE

## I. INTRODUCTION

The issue of proximate cause only arises after the plaintiff has proven that the defendant's negligence was the cause in fact of the plaintiff's injury. The doctrine limits liability for the effects of the defendant's negligence based on a policy determination that the defendant should not automatically be held liable for all the improbable and far reaching consequences of an act.

## II. UNFORESEEABLE CONSEQUENCES

### A. Foreseeability

1. Generally
   The majority of jurisdictions will hold a defendant liable for the results of negligent conduct only if the results were reasonably foreseeable. Both the type of damage and the specific plaintiff must be reasonably foreseeable. See Chief Judge Cardozo's opinion in *Palsgraf v. Long Island R.R. Co.*

2. Exceptions to Foreseeability Rule

   Mnemonic: **MEDIC**

   a. Unforeseeable **M**anner
      One is liable for foreseeable harm that occurs in an unforeseeable manner.

      Example:
      An asbestos cement cover is dropped into a boiling vat of chemicals, placing others at risk of injury from the splash of the chemicals, but no one is actually hurt. A short time later the cover explodes and a plaintiff is hurt by the resulting splash (foreseeable injury caused in an unforeseeable manner).

b. Extent of Damages
One is liable for the unforeseeable extent of damages if they result from a foreseeable type of injury.

c. Improbability
Injury which is only remotely likely is considered foreseeable for purposes of liability.

d. Plaintiff Class
Even if injury to a particular plaintiff is not foreseeable, liability may be imposed if the plaintiff is a member of a class which could foreseeably be injured.

Example:
Two boats crash into a bridge and the debris clogs the river. As a result, the backed up water floods the plaintiff's land. The landowners are held to be a foreseeable class. See *Petition of Kinsman Transit Co.* (Kinsman No. 1)

B.    Direct Causation
The minority of jurisdictions will hold a defendant liable for all the direct consequences of negligent conduct, regardless of whether the consequences are foreseeable.

III.   INTERVENING CAUSES

A.    Generally
An intervening cause is an action by a different party or entity that occurs after a defendant's negligent action and contributes to the plaintiff's injury. The main issue is whether the intervening cause breaks the chain of causation such that the original defendant is no longer liable.

B.    Foreseeable Intervening Cause
Where the acts of the intervening party are foreseeable, or the kind of harm suffered by the plaintiff is foreseeable, the defendant is not relieved of liability.

Examples of foreseeable intervening causes:

1. Responses to Danger
   Responses to a dangerous situation created by the defendant are generally considered foreseeable intervening causes. For example, a defendant who created a dangerous situation would be liable for injuries incurred during:

   a. a reasonable escape attempt,

   b. a rescue effort, or

   c. an attempt to provide medical treatment.

2. Negligence of Intervening Party
   The negligence of a third party is generally a foreseeable intervening cause. Such is the case when it is the risk of negligence by the third party that makes the original party's conduct negligent. For example, one who sells liquor to an intoxicated person, knowing that the person will subsequently drive a car, will be liable for the consequences of the intoxicated person's negligent driving. Note, this usually applies to tavern keepers, and not to social hosts.

3. Subsequent Disease or Accident
   If one's negligent act causes another to be more susceptible to disease or further accident, the negligent actor is liable for the consequences of the subsequent intervening disease or accident.

C. Superseding Intervening Cause
   If the intervening act is not foreseeable, it is a superseding cause such that the original negligent defendant may be relieved of liability for the damages caused by the intervening party.

Examples of superseding intervening causes:

1. Malicious Acts
   Intentional, malicious or criminal conduct by a third party is sufficiently unforeseeable to relieve a defendant of liability.

2. Gross or Extraordinary Negligence
   While ordinary negligence by a third party is considered foreseeable, extraordinary negligence is not and may relieve a defendant of liability.

3. Acts of Nature
   Acts of nature, also known as acts of God, are unforeseeable, and will relieve a defendant of liability if the damage caused is different than that which was threatened by the defendant.

4. Suicide
   Suicide is a superseding intervening cause if the person who committed suicide was not driven by an irresistible impulse.

## IV. SHIFTING RESPONSIBILITY

Sometimes a negligent actor will be relieved of liability if responsibility for the dangerous situation passes to a third party. Though there is no general rule stating when responsibility will pass from one party to another, the courts will generally consider whether:

A.    the actor's negligence was a substantial cause of the plaintiff's injury,

B.    the actor's negligence was of a continuing nature,

C.    the injury incurred was of the same type expected to result from the actor's negligence, and

D.    the actor should reasonably have foreseen the negligence of the third party.

## CASE CLIPS

**Larrimore v. American National Insurance Co. (1939)** Ke
**Facts:** The plaintiff was injured by an exploding can of rat poison placed near a stove by his employer. A state statute prohibited storage of rat poison in an unsafe place.
**Issue:** Is one liable for neglecting a duty imposed by statute?
**Rule:** One is liable for neglecting a duty imposed by statute only when the injury is of the kind that the statute is designed to protect against.

**Overseas Tankship (U.K.) Ltd. v.**
**Morts Dock & Engineering Co., Ltd.**
**"Wagon Mound No. 1" (1961)** Ke, Ep, Fr
**Facts:** A vessel owned by Overseas Tankership negligently discharged oil which caused minor damage to a wharf owned by Morts Dock. Further, the oil ignited causing severe damage to the wharf.
**Issue:** Is a party liable for damages that arise directly from its negligent act if they are not reasonably foreseeable?
**Rule:** One is not liable for unlikely and unforeseeable results of a negligent act, even if they are direct.
**Note:** This case expressly rejects the rule set forth in In re Polemis.

**Palsgraf v. Long Island R.R. Co. (1928)** Ke, Ep, Fr
**Facts:** A railroad employee pushed a man from behind, hoping to help him board a moving train. The man dropped his package, causing the fireworks contained within to explode. The explosion caused scales at the other end of the platform to fall, injuring Palsgraf.
**Issue:** Is one liable for damages to an unforeseeable third party resulting from one's negligent acts toward a second party?
**Rule:** An actor owes no duty of care to unforeseeable plaintiffs, and thus is not liable to an unforeseeable plaintiff for damages resulting from a negligent act toward another.
**Dissent:** An actor has a duty to the public at large. An actor who commits a wrongful act is liable not only to those who would likely be injured by the act, but to all whose injuries are in fact proximately caused by the act.

**Note:** Chief Judge Cardozo, addressing the question as an issue of duty, never reaches the question of proximate cause as does Judge Andrews in the dissent.

### Dellwo v. Pearson (1961) Ke

**Facts:** The defendant, age 12, drove a motorboat over the plaintiff's fishing line, shattering the plaintiff's reel. A piece of the reel struck the plaintiff's glasses, causing an eye injury.

**Issue:** Is one's negligence the proximate cause of an injury when the injury is an unforeseeable result of the negligent act?

**Rule:** Negligence is judged by foresight, while proximate cause is judged by hindsight. Proximate cause exists whether or not the actor could have foreseen the outcome of the negligent act. There is no foreseeability requirement for proximate cause.

### Watson v. Rheinderknecht (1901) Ke

**Facts:** The plaintiff was injured by the defendant's assault and battery. The plaintiff was especially sensitive because of prior injuries suffered while serving in the army.

**Issue:** May a party recover for an injury that was especially severe because of prior trauma?

**Rule:** A party is liable for the direct and immediate consequences of its negligent acts, including the aggravation of an existing injury.

### Wagner v. International Ry. Co. (1921) Ke, Ep

**Facts:** Wagner's cousin was thrown from a door left open on the defendant's train after the train suddenly swayed. Wagner was killed while attempting to rescue his cousin.

**Issue:** Is a party whose negligence placed another in peril liable for injuries suffered by rescuers?

**Rule:** Since it is foreseeable that rescuers will attempt to assist a person in peril, the party which placed the person in peril is liable for injuries sustained by the rescuers.

### McLaughlin v. Mine Safety Appliance Co. (1962) Ke, Fr

**Facts:** McLaughlin was burned when a firefighter tried to warm her with heating blocks. The block's manufacturer had posted a warning on the wrapping, but not on the item itself, and had demonstrated proper use of the blocks, which the firefighter ignored.

**Issue:** Is a negligent manufacturer liable for injuries despite the negligence of the person using the products?

**Rule:** Gross negligence in the use of a product is a superseding intervening cause relieving a manufacturer of liability for its negligence.

### Godesky v. Provo City (1984) Ke

**Facts:** Godesky was electrocuted when, at his boss' instruction, he grabbed an uninsulated wire owned by the defendant.

**Issue:** Does an intervening negligent act automatically become a superseding cause, relieving the original actor of liability?

**Rule:** A foreseeable intervening negligent act does not become a superseding cause that relieves the original actor of liability. The foreseeable intervening negligence is a concurrent cause.

### Newlin v. The New England Telephone & Telegraph Co. (1944) Ke

**Facts:** The New England Telephone and Telegraph Company's negligently maintained telephone pole fell on a power line, cutting off Newlin's cooling system and killing his mushrooms.

**Issue:** Is a party liable for all the results of its negligent acts?

**Rule:** A party is liable for all damages that are the proximate result of its negligence. Proximate cause does not involve foresight.

### Stevenson v. East Ohio Gas Co. (1946) Ke

**Facts:** Stevenson sued to recover eight days of lost wages because he was unable to enter his workplace due to an explosion and fire caused by the defendant's negligence.

**Issue:** Is a party liable when it's negligence causes an unintentional interference with a contract between two other parties?

**Rule:** Liability to others not in privity with a negligent actor is limited to physical injuries or physical property damages; it does not extend to the loss of wages or other economic losses.

### Union Oil Co. v. Oppen (1974) Ke

**Facts:** Union Oil Company's oil drilling operations caused an oil spill which killed a large number of fish, causing economic losses to the plaintiff, a commercial fisher.

**Issue:** Does a cause of action lie for loss of prospective income caused by a defendant's negligence?

**Rule:** Foreseeable economic losses may be recovered in a negligence action.

### Dillon v. Legg (1968) Ke, Ep

**Facts:** Dillon suffered great emotional injury when she saw her daughter killed by Legg's negligent driving. Her safety was at no time endangered.

**Issue:** Can one recover for emotional trauma caused by witnessing the death of a close relative if one does not fear for one's own safety?

**Rule:** In an action for emotional distress, factors such as proximity to the "zone of danger" and the relationship to the physically injured party may be considered in allowing for recovery.

### Ryan v. New York Central R.R. Co. (1866) Ep

**Facts:** The Railroad Company negligently burned its own woodshed. The fire spread and burned Ryan's house.

**Issue:** What factors distinguish proximate damages of an accident (recoverable) from remote damages of an accident (not recoverable)?

**Rule:** Proximate damages are the anticipated, ordinary, natural, and necessary consequences of an accident. Remote damages do not necessarily follow from the occurrence of an accident, but rather result from accidental and varying circumstances.

### Gorris v. Scott (1874) Ep

**Facts:** The plaintiff's sheep were washed overboard from the defendant's ship. Had the defendant complied with health statutes, the sheep would not have been lost.

**Issue:** Is a statutory violation alone sufficient evidence to prove a defendant's negligence?

**Rule:** To invoke a violation of a statute as evidence of negligence, the plaintiff must show that the injury sustained was of the type the statute was intended to prevent.

### Berry v. The Borough of Sugar Notch (1899) Ep

**Facts:** Berry, a train engineer, was injured when a tree fell on him as the train he operated passed underneath the tree at a rate in excess of a local speeding ordinance. The borough of Sugar Notch had been negligent in maintaining the tree.

**Issue:** Does a plaintiff's statutory violation at the time of a defendant's negligence bar the plaintiff from recovery of damages?

**Rule:** A plaintiff's statutory violation will not bar a plaintiff from recovering if the violation was not the cause of the accident, and did not contribute to it.

### Brower v. New York Central & H.R.R. (1918) Ep

**Facts:** The defendant's negligence in its operation of a train crossing caused Brower's horse and wagon to be destroyed in a train collision. The driver of the wagon was stunned and unable to stop thieves from stealing merchandise that was in the wagon.

**Issue:** If a defendant's negligence causes an accident, is it also the proximate cause of the theft of property which occurs after the accident?

**Rule:** When negligence leaves a person unable to protect one's property, it is foreseeable that the property will be stolen. Thus, the party's negligence is the proximate cause of the property loss.

### In Re Arbitration Between Polemis and Furness, Withy and Co., Ltd. (1921) Ep, Fr

**Facts:** The defendant chartered a vessel from the plaintiff to transport chemicals. The defendant's negligent handling of a plank on the ship created a spark. The resulting explosion destroyed the plaintiff's ship.

**Issue:** Is a person liable for those consequences of a negligent act that are not reasonably foreseeable?

**Rule:** One is liable for all direct results of one's negligence regardless of whether the type of injury could have been anticipated.

**Note:** This case was later rejected by Wagon Mound No. 1.

### Marshall v. Nugent (1955) Ep

**Facts:** A defendant forced Marshall's car off the road, offered to help get the car back on the road, and suggested that the driver of the car warn oncoming traffic. As the driver of the car tried to give warning, Nugent lost control of his oncoming car and hit him.

**Issue:** If a person is rendered vulnerable to further injury by a party's negligence, is the negligent party liable for the further injuries which result?

**Rule:** An injury that is a foreseeable result of a negligent act is not a superseding intervening cause. The defendant is liable to the plaintiff for such an injury.

### Weirum v. RKO General, Inc. (1975) Ep

**Facts:** A radio station sponsored a contest giving prizes to the first person to find its disc jockey at different locations in the city. The plaintiff was killed by a driver who was speeding to reach the disc jockey's location.

**Issue:** If one's conduct encourages a negligent response by another, is the party liable for the other's negligence?

**Rule:** If it is foreseeable that a party's conduct will cause others to behave in a negligent and dangerous manner, that party will not be relieved of liability by the intervening negligence of another.

### Steinhauser v. Hertz Corp. (1970) Fr

**Facts:** Steinhauser's schizophrenic tendencies were severely aggravated by a car accident which resulted from the defendant's negligence.

**Issue:** Is a negligent actor liable for aggravating an underlying illness?

**Rule:** An actor who negligently aggravates a pre-existing illness is liable, but damages should be lower than if the actor had caused the illness originally.

### Petition of Kinsman Transit Co. (1964)
### "Kinsman No. 1" Fr

**Facts:** Employees of Kinsman Transit negligently moored a boat. The boat broke loose due to pressure from floating ice and floated downstream. The ship hit another ship and both crashed into a city-owned drawbridge, clogging up the river and causing a flood on plaintiffs' property.

**Issue:** Is a negligent party liable for completely unforeseeable damages?

**Rule:** Unforeseeability of the exact developments and of the extent of loss will not limit liability if the damages are the consequence of the same risk which made the original act negligent and are of the same general sort which was expected.

# Chapter 8

## COMPENSATION FOR HARM

### I. ACTUAL DAMAGES

Unlike intentional torts, there are no nominal damages awarded for negligence. A plaintiff has to show actual damages as part of a cause of action. This usually includes a required showing of some physical injury.

### II. TYPES OF RECOVERABLE DAMAGES

A plaintiff who has sustained some physical injury may recover damages for all the harm sustained, which may include:

A. Medical Expenses

B. Lost Earnings

C. Future Earnings
The jury will often hear expert testimony regarding the value of the lost earning capacity and will approximate the value of future earnings lost, taking inflation and interest rates into account.

D. Pain and Suffering
Includes both amount of pain suffered up to the time of trial and an estimate of future pain.

E. Mental Distress
Includes fear and shock when injured, humiliation from disfigurement, impairment of activities, and anxiety over new life.

F. Property Damages
Can be measured either by the cost to repair the damaged item, or if repair is not possible, the fair market value of the destroyed property.

## III.    NONRECOVERABLE DAMAGES

A.    Interest
One may not recover the interest which would have been earned on monetary damages from the date of the accident to the date of the verdict.

B.    Attorney's Fees

## IV.    TAXATION AND DAMAGES

A.    Tax Free
Damages for personal injuries are tax free, regardless of whether damages are awarded by a court judgment or received as part of a private settlement. Courts are split on the issue of whether a defendant is allowed to tell the jury that damages are tax free.

B.    Calculation of Damages and Taxation

    1. Past Earnings
    Calculations for lost past earnings are based on the plaintiff's net earnings.

    2. Future Earnings
    Lost future earnings are calculated according to the plaintiff's tax bracket.

        a. Ordinary Taxpayer — at gross

        b. High Income Taxpayer — at net

        c. Federal Rule — regardless of tax bracket, always based on net

## V.    COLLATERAL SOURCE RULE

The amount of damages is not reduced if the plaintiff recovered, or could recover compensation from other sources such as insurance, disability benefits, or social security. Even if the plaintiff receives free medical care, the defendant has to compensate the plaintiff for the reasonable value of those benefits.

Rationale:

A.   The plaintiff prepaid to receive these benefits. E.g., It would be unfair to reduce a plaintiff's damages because the plaintiff has paid insurance premiums for numerous years.

B.   Even if the plaintiff did not prepay, it is not right to aid the defendant who is a tortfeasor.

C.   In many cases, the plaintiff is obligated to pay for the benefits received from a third party, such as an insurance company, out of the damages award. This is called subrogation.

## VI.   MITIGATION OF DAMAGES

A plaintiff cannot recover damages for injuries which a reasonably prudent person would have avoided. Usually this only applies to conduct after the accident. Some courts also look to conduct before the accident and will reduce damages because of a plaintiff's failure to take adequate precautions to reduce potential damages.

## VII.   PUNITIVE DAMAGES

Punitive damages are awarded as a punishment, meaning that they are always in excess of the actual harm suffered. They are only awarded in cases where a defendant has acted recklessly, wantonly, or willfully.

## VIII.   WRONGFUL DEATH AND SURVIVAL

A.   Under Common Law

1. A plaintiff's action against a defendant was extinguished when the plaintiff died.

2. Third parties that were harmed by a plaintiff's death were barred from bringing an action. Thus, there was no recovery in tort available to a plaintiff's survivors.

B.   Statutory Changes

1. Survival Statutes
Survival statutes allow a decedent's cause of action to be continued by the decedent's estate. They allow recovery for the harm that the decedent suffered before death. This includes pain and suffering, medical care, lost income, etc.

2. Wrongful Death Statutes
Wrongful death statutes allow a decedent's survivors to assert an action for damages based on the decedent's death. They allow recovery for damages that occurred after death. The survivors can sue for grief, loss of companionship, etc.

Note: Any defenses that a defendant could have asserted against the decedent can also be used against the survivors.

3. Exception
Torts that invade a very personal interest will not survive death, e.g., defamation, invasion of privacy, etc.

# CASE CLIPS

**Christopher v. United States (1965)** Ke
**Facts:**  Christopher sought damages under the Federal Tort Claims Act for paralysis resulting from negligent treatment in a Veteran's Administration Hospital.
**Issue:** What types of compensation are available to an injured person?
**Rule:**   An injured plaintiff can recover for pain and suffering, past and future lost income, and medical expenses.

### Jackson v. Johns-Manville Corp. (1986) Ke

**Facts:** Jackson suffered from asbestosis poisoning and established at trial that persons with asbestosis poisoning would likely get cancer.

**Issue:** May a plaintiff recover damages for the medical probability of developing an illness?

**Rule:** Once an injury becomes actionable (i.e., once some effect appears), a plaintiff can recover for the medical probability of developing an illness.

### Feldman v. Allegheny Airlines, Inc. (1975) Ke

**Facts:** A lower court ruled that inflation could be considered in calculating the damages for Feldman, who was killed in a plane crash.

**Issue:** May inflation be considered in assessing damages?

**Rule:** A court may include anticipated inflation in its damages award.

### Murphy v. Martin Oil Co. (1974) Ke

**Facts:** Murphy brought both wrongful death and survivor actions after her husband died in a fire.

**Issue:** Can surviving spouses recover under both wrongful death and survivor statutes?

**Rule:** Surviving spouses can recover under both wrongful death and survivor statutes for the death of their spouse. To avoid double recovery, the latter is usually limited to compensation for lost wages and pain and suffering from the time of the accident to the time of death, while the former compensates for the future loss of the spouse.

### Cassano v. Durham (1981) Ke

**Facts:** Cassano asserted a wrongful death action after her lover died.

**Issue:** Can one who maintained a "live-in" relationship without marrying the decedent bring a wrongful death action?

**Rule:** A live-in plaintiff cannot be classified as a "surviving spouse" under intestacy laws. One must be legally married to assert an action under these acts.

### Borer v. American Airlines, Inc. (1977) Ke

**Facts:** Borer was injured by the defendant's negligence. Her children sued the defendant for loss of parental consortium.

**Issue:** May children sue to recover damages for the loss of the services, companionship, affection and guidance of a parent?

**Rule:** There is no common law recovery by a child for the loss of parental consortium.
**Note:** The courts will allow a spouse to sue for loss of consortium.

### Sullivan v. Old Colony Street Ry. (1908) Ep
**Facts:** No facts stated.
**Rule:** Damage awards are monetary compensation for actual loss.

### Zibbell v. Southern Pacific Co. (1911) Ep
**Facts:** No facts stated.
**Rule:** "No rational being would change places with the injured man for an amount of gold that would fill the room of the court, yet no lawyer would contend that such is not the legal measure of damages."

### McDougald v. Garber (1989) Ep, Fr
**Facts:** During surgery, McDougald suffered severe brain damage, resulting in a permanent comatose condition. McDougald was awarded nonpecuniary damages for conscious pain and suffering as well as for loss of the pleasures and pursuits of life.
**Issue 1:** Is some degree of cognitive awareness a prerequisite to recovery for loss of enjoyment of life?
**Rule 1:** There must be some level of cognitive awareness by the plaintiff to recover for loss of enjoyment of life.
**Issue 2:** May damages for loss of enjoyment of life be considered separately from pain and suffering?
**Rule 2:** When considering nonpecuniary damage awards, compensation for loss of enjoyment of life is included as part of compensation for pain and suffering.

### O'Shea v. Riverway Towing Co. (1982) Ep
**Facts:** O'Shea fell while leaving the defendant's boat.
**Issue:** May inflation be computed when calculating lost future wages?
**Rule:** Inflation should be considered when computing lost future wages, but its effects should be balanced against interest earned on the settlement because inflation rates and interest rates are related.

### Firestone v. Crown Center Redevelopment Corp. (1985) Ep
**Facts:** Firestone was injured due to the defendant's negligent construction of a skywalk and was awarded $15,000,000 in damages.

Missouri law required Firestone to file a remittitur of $2,250,000 to prevent the ordering of a new trial. This procedure was used in cases where a judge decided an excessive verdict was given against the weight of the evidence.

**Issue:** May a court require plaintiffs to diminish their damage awards, under the doctrine of remittitur, where the judge decided the verdict was excessive given the weight of the evidence?

**Rule:** The doctrine of remittitur is abolished. Judges may grant new trials, but may not require plaintiffs to diminish their damage awards where the judge decides the verdict was excessive.

### Norfolk & Western Ry. Co. v. Liepelt (1980) Ep

**Facts:** In a wrongful death suit the trial court refused to allow the jury to be told that damages would be tax free.

**Issue:** Must a judge inform jurors that a plaintiff's damages award for a personal injury will be tax free?

**Rule:** A judge must permit a defendant to inform the jury that damages received in a personal injury award are not taxable.

**Note:** Courts are divided on this issue.

### Wilbur v. Kerr (1982) Ep

**Facts:** Wilbur fathered a child after undergoing a vasectomy that was performed by Kerr.

**Issue:** May parents recover for the expenses of raising a child that was born because of a doctor's negligence in performing a sterilization operation?

**Rule:** Parents may not recover for the expense of a child born after a negligently performed sterilization.

### McGinley v. United States (1971) Ep

**Facts:** McGinley refused to undergo surgery to alleviate pain incurred by an accident for which the defendant was responsible.

**Issue:** Does the duty to mitigate damages require that the injured party take all possible actions to alleviate its injuries?

**Rule:** A plaintiff has a duty to submit to reasonable medical treatment only; the test of reasonableness is determined by a jury.

### Harding v. Town of Townshend (1871) Ep

**Facts:** The trial court allowed the defendant's liability for damages to be reduced by the amount of money the plaintiff received from his insurance company.

**Issue:** Can testimony that a plaintiff was compensated from collateral sources be admitted in trial?

**Rule:** A court may not allow into evidence the fact that a plaintiff received payments from collateral sources.

### Fischer v. Johns-Manville Corporation (1986) Ep, Fr

**Facts:** Fischer sued to recover damages for lung disease suffered as a result of exposure to asbestos supplied by the defendants.

**Issue:** May punitive damages be awarded in products liability actions?

**Rule:** Punitive damages may be awarded in a products liability action when a manufacturer, aware of a risk inherent in its product, fails to warn of such risk, and fails to act to reduce the risk.

### Seffert v. Los Angeles Transit Lines (1961) Fr

**Facts:** The defendant's bus doors closed on Seffert, dragging her some distance. Seffert was awarded $187,903.75 in damages.

**Issue:** When can an appellate court reduce the amount of a verdict?

**Rule:** An appellate court can reduce a verdict only if it shocks the conscience and necessarily implies that the verdict must have been the result of passion and prejudice. An award will not be reduced just because it seems excessive.

### Taylor v. Superior Court (1979) Fr

**Facts:** Taylor was injured when he was struck by a car driven by an intoxicated driver who had numerous drunken driving convictions.

**Issue:** Does driving while intoxicated fulfill the malice requirement that is necessary to receive an award of punitive damages?

**Rule:** Malice implies an act conceived in a spirit of mischief or with criminal indifference towards obligations owed to others. Driving while intoxicated fulfills this malice requirement.

# Chapter 9

## THE IMPACT OF INSURANCE

### I.  LIABILITY INSURANCE

A.  Impact on Doctrine
The availability of liability insurance has led to the abolishment of several doctrines, such as the doctrine of sovereign immunity and the doctrine of charitable immunity.

B.  Insurance Companies

1. An insurance company is liable for both compensatory and punitive damages assessed against its insured.

2. An insurance company can be liable for an entire judgment if it does not act in good faith to settle claims within policy limits when there is a substantial likelihood of a verdict in excess of the policy limits.

### II.  COLLATERAL SOURCE RULE

A tortfeasor may not introduce evidence to prove that a plaintiff has been compensated by an independent collateral source such as insurance, pension, continued wages, or disability payments.

### III.  SUBROGATION AGREEMENTS

In the absense of a subrogation agreement between an insurer and an insured, an insurer that has paid medical or hospital expense benefits has no right to share in the proceeds of the insured's recovery against a tortfeasor.

## CASE CLIPS

### Hicks v. State (1975) Ke
**Facts:** Hicks brought a wrongful death action, asserting the state's negligent failure to maintain a bridge.
**Issue:** Is the state protected from negligence suits by the doctrine of "sovereign immunity?"
**Rule:** The doctrine of sovereign immunity is abolished.

### Pierce v. Yakima Valley Memorial Hospital Association (1953) Ke
**Facts:** The plaintiff brought a malpractice action against a charitable hospital in which he was a paying patient.
**Issue:** Is a charitable organization immune from liability for injuries caused by the negligent conduct of its employees?
**Rule:** The doctrine of charitable immunity is abolished.

### Harrell v. Travelers Indemnity Co. (1977) Ke
**Facts:** The plaintiff recovered compensatory and punitive damages for injuries caused by the reckless drunk driving of Travelers' client. Travelers refused to pay the punitive damages award.
**Issue:** Is an insurance company liable for punitive damages?
**Rule:** An insurance company is liable for both compensatory and punitive damages assessed against its insured.

### Ryan v. New York Central R.R. Co. (1866) Ke
**Facts:** The Railroad Company carelessly burned its own woodshed. The fire spread and burned Ryan's house.
**Issue:** What factors distinguish proximate damages of an accident (recoverable) from remote damages of an accident (not recoverable)?
**Rule:** Proximate damages are the anticipated, ordinary, natural, and necessary consequence of an accident. Remote damages do not necessarily follow from the occurrence of an accident, but rather result from accidental and varying circumstances.

### Helfend v. Southern California Rapid Transit Dist. (1970) Ke
**Facts:** Helfend was awarded general and special damages for injuries sustained in an accident. Part of his medical expenses were paid by insurance.

**Issue:** Should a tortfeasor, in an effort to reduce a damage award, be allowed to present the jury with evidence that the plaintiff has already been partially compensated?

**Rule:** A tortfeasor may not introduce evidence to prove that a plaintiff has been compensated by an independent collateral source such as insurance, pension, continued wages, or disability payments. This is an application of the "collateral source rule."

### Johansen v. California State Automobile Association Inter-Insurance Bureau (1975) Ke

**Facts:** Johansen, injured by the defendant's insured, offered to settle his claim for the defendant's $10,000 policy limit. Despite Johansen's strong case, the defendant refused to settle and lost in court.

**Issue:** Can punitive damages be assessed against an insurance company for failing to settle a claim within policy limits if there is a substantial likelihood of a recovery in excess of those limits?

**Rule:** An insurer can be liable for an entire judgment if it does not act in good faith to settle claims within policy limits when there is a substantial likelihood of a verdict in excess of those limits.

### Bartlett v. Travelers Insurance Co. (1933) Ke

**Facts:** Travelers settled the claims of two of three people injured in an accident caused by their insured. The third obtained a verdict equal to the policy limit. Travelers offered to pay the difference between the policy limit and the amounts already paid to the other two persons.

**Issue:** Is an insurance company that faces multiple claims arising from a single accident permitted to settle some, but not all of the claims?

**Rule:** An insurer is allowed to settle some of the claims that arise out of a multi-party action. If it has acted reasonably and in good faith it is not liable for the full amount of judgments received by the remaining claimants. At most it must pay the difference between the policy limit and the money paid out in settlement.

### Crisci v. Security Insurance Co. (1967) Ep, Fr

**Facts:** Crisci was sued by her tenant, but agreed to a settlement. Security, her insurance company, refused to pay the settlement amount which was within the policy limit, even though it knew that she would probably lose in court. The case went to court and she lost.

**Issue:** Is an insurer liable for an award in excess of its policy limit if the insurer acted in bad faith by refusing a reasonable settlement?

**Rule:** An insurer is liable for a judgment in excess of a policy limit if it acted in bad faith.

### Frost v. Porter Leasing Corp. (1982) Fr

**Facts:** Frost received a $250,000 lump sum settlement for a tort claim. He had previously received $22,700 in medical expense benefits under a union health plan paid for by his employer.

**Issue:** Does an insurer have a right of subrogation to share in the proceeds recovered by its insured in a lawsuit?

**Rule:** In the absence of a subrogation agreement between an insurer and an insured, an insurer that has paid medical or hospital expense benefits has no right to share in the proceeds of the insured's recovery against a tortfeasor.

### Lalomia v. Bankers & Shippers Ins. Co. (1970) Fr

**Facts:** Lalomia's wife was killed in a collision between her car and a motorized bicycle driven by a 12-year-old boy. Lalomia sued the insurance company of the boy's father, claiming that he was negligent in allowing his minor son to operate such a dangerous vehicle.

**Issue:** Does a homeowner's insurance policy which covers damages caused by the insured to the person or property of others cover injuries that are caused by the insured's negligent conduct?

**Rule:** A homeowner's insurance policy covers damages arising out of the negligent behavior of the insured policyholder.

## Chapter 10

## IMPUTED LIABILITY

I. **VICARIOUS LIABILITY**

The doctrine of vicarious liability imputes the wrongful conduct of a tortfeasor to a third person who is considered to be responsible for the tortfeasor's actions. This responsibility arises out of a special relationship, e.g., in employment relationships, family relationships or joint ventures.

One of the motivating factors of this doctrine is the need to find a defendant who can compensate the plaintiff.

A. Respondeat Superior

1. Employer-Employee
Under the doctrine of respondeat superior, an employer is liable for the torts that employees commit while acting within the scope of their employment. An employee is considered to be a worker who is subject to the control of the employer.

2. Scope of Employment
All actions that are closely connected to an employee's work which are done with a purpose to advance an employer's business interests are within the scope of employment.

Actions that are expressly prohibited by an employer are not automatically outside the scope of employment. Rather, the court will consider both the fact that they were prohibited, and whether they were performed for the employer's benefit.

a. Commuting to Work
Travelling between work and home is outside the scope of employment.

b. Frolic and Personal Detours During Business Trips

    i.  Traditionally, an employer was liable only if the accident occurred while an employee was on the way back to the business route after ending the personal visit.

    ii.  Today, courts will hold an employer liable if the detour is reasonably foreseeable. One factor to consider in foreseeability is the distance of the detour.

3. Intentional Torts
An employer is liable for intentional torts by an employee if they were done for the benefit of the employer's business. However, if an employee acted for personal reasons, the employer is not liable. Some courts allow liability only if the intentional tort was reasonably foreseeable by the employer.

B.  Independent Contractors
Independent contractors are workers who are not subject to the control of the employer. They decide for themselves how to do the work.

An employer is not held liable for a tort committed by an independent contractor unless:

Mnemonic: **NUN**

1. **N**ondelegable
Public policy makes the duty nondelegable;

2. **U**ltrahazardous
The work involves ultrahazardous activities; or

3. **N**egligence
An employer negligently selects an incompetent independent contractor.

C.  Joint Enterprise
All members of a joint venture are vicariously liable for the torts of each other.

Mnemonic: **MAC**

1.  **M**utuality of Control
Each member must have an equal say on the issue of how things are done. This is not necessarily equal physical control, but at least a situation where all have equal influence.

2.  **A**greement
The members must be acting in concert by some express or implied agreement.

3.  **C**ommon Pecuniary Purpose
All the members must have a common pecuniary purpose. Merely sharing expenses or a social interest is not enough.

D.  Bailments and Other Bases

1.  Automobile Owner and Driver
Generally, an automobile owner is not vicariously liable for the conduct of another person who drives the car.

However, this rule is subject to exceptions:

a.  Permissive Use/Auto Consent Statutes
Some states have enacted statutes that make a car owner vicariously liable for the tortious conduct of any person that drives the car with the owner's consent. Of course the driver has to act reasonably within the scope of the owner's consent, e.g., Rob lends his car to Susan to go to a movie, then Susan drives 2,000 miles: no consent.

If an owner lends a car to a driver who in turn lends it to another, the owner will be liable for damages by the second driver if the first driver was in the car at the time of the accident.

    b.  Family Purpose

       In the absence of a statute, some courts will hold an owner of a family car vicariously liable for the torts committed by immediate family or household members driving with express or implied permission. A family purpose exists anytime any family member benefits from the use of the car.

    c.  Bailee

       If there is no permissive use statute, a bailor is not vicariously liable for a bailee's negligent conduct unless the bailor was negligent in allowing the bailment.

2.  Parent-Child

Parents are usually not vicariously liable for the negligence of their children.

Exceptions:

    a.  The parent was negligent.

    b.  The child was acting as a family agent.

## II.    IMPUTED CONTRIBUTORY NEGLIGENCE

Contributory negligence can be vicariously transferred between parties just like ordinary negligence.

For example, Susan, Brett's employee, is involved in an accident with Rob. If Susan is contributorily negligent, Brett is also considered to have been contributorily negligent. Thus, Brett would be barred from recovery for damages to his car in an action against Rob.

However, in situations where vicarious liability exists because of consent statutes or the family purpose doctrine, the courts will usually not impute contributory negligence.

## CASE CLIPS

**Ira S. Bushey & Sons, Inc. v. United States (1968)** Ke, Ep
**Facts:** An inebriated Coast Guard sailor returning to his ship from shore leave accidently damaged the plaintiff's drydock controls.
**Issue:** Can an employer be vicariously liable for torts committed by an employee which were not made to further the employer's interest?
**Rule:** An employer will be held vicariously liable for foreseeable torts which are committed by employees, even if the torts do not occur while the employer's interest was being advanced.

### Becker v. Interstate Properties (1977) Ke
**Facts:** Becker was injured in a construction accident caused by the defendant's subcontractor, who was not properly insured.
**Issue:** May an employer be held vicariously liable for the torts of an independent subcontractor?
**Rule:** An employer may be held vicariously liable for the torts of an independent subcontractor if the employer did not exercise ordinary care in selecting the subcontractor.

### Jackson v. Jackson (1974) Ke
**Facts:** Jackson brought an action for malicious prosecution against the partners of the law firm representing her estranged husband.
**Issue:** Are all partners in a law firm liable for the actions of one of the partners in the law firm?
**Rule:** Partners are held vicariously liable for wrongful acts by other partners which are in furtherance of business.
**Note:** Actions such as malicious prosecution are not considered in furtherance of a law firm's business.

### Howard v. Zimmerman (1926) Ke
**Facts:** The defendant borrowed his father's car and went for a joyride with his friend. His friend drove the car negligently and hit the plaintiff.
**Issue:** May a person who is not in an authority position over a party be held vicariously liable for the negligence of that party?
**Rule:** When two persons are involved in a joint enterprise with equal authority and a common goal, one can be held vicariously liable for the negligence of the other.

## Weber v. Stokely-Van Camp Inc. (1966) Ke

**Facts:** The plaintiff was injured in a car accident when his employee, who was driving for business reasons, negligently hit another car. The driver of the other car was also negligent.

**Issue:** Must contributory negligence be imputed between two parties who have a relationship that would give rise to vicarious liability?

**Rule:** Contributory negligence is not imputed between two parties if the party who is vicariously liable does not control the other party's minute to minute decisions.

## Hardy v. Brantley (1985) Ep

**Facts:** Plaintiff was killed when his perforated duodenal ulcer was misdiagnosed by an emergency room physician and went untreated.

**Issue:** When can a provider of services be held vicariously liable for the conduct of its agents?

**Rule:** A provider of services is vicariously liable for the conduct of its agents when a person engages the services promoted by the provider without regard to the identity of the agent who is contracted to provide that service. The injuries must be proximately caused by the negligence of the agent.

# Chapter 11

## STRICT LIABILITY

I.  HARM CAUSED BY ANIMALS

A.  Trespassing Animals
    If an animal trespasses on a plaintiff's land and causes damages, the animal's owner is strictly liable. However, if the owner is walking the animal along a public road and it strays onto the adjoining land, the owner is not strictly liable.

B.  Dangerous Animals
    An owner is strictly liable for any harm that a dangerous animal causes if:

    1. the harm results from a dangerous propensity which is characteristic of the animal's species or a dangerous propensity particular to the animal that the owner knew or should have known; and

    2. the victim did not contribute to the animal's behavior.

C.  Domestic Animals
    An owner is strictly liable only if the owner knew or should have known that the animal had dangerous propensities.

    First Bite Rule
    The owner is liable for the second time that the animal bites somebody but not for the first time it bites if it never showed such a propensity to bite before.

II. ULTRAHAZARDOUS ACTIVITIES

    There is strict liability for activities that involve an inherent and substantial risk of harm. Generally, if a defendant engages in such an activity, the defendant is strictly liable for any harm caused.

A.    Limitations

    1. Strict liability extends only to foreseeable plaintiffs who are injured by a kind of risk that made the activity ultrahazardous.

    For example, radiation is the foreseeable risk of a nuclear reactor. However, if a wall of the reactor collapses because of an earthquake strict liability would not be applied because that is not the risk that makes a reactor dangerous.

    2. The defendant is not liable if the plaintiff is hurt because of the plaintiff's abnormal sensitivity.

B.    Determination
Some factors to consider when determining whether an activity is ultrahazardous are:

    1. the degree of risk of harm to persons or property.

    2. the seriousness of the harm that could result.

    3. whether the activity cannot be performed with complete safety.

    4. whether the activity is commonly engaged in.

    5. the location at which the activity is performed.

    6. the value to the community v. the activity's dangerous attributes.

C.    Examples
Some examples of ultrahazardous activities include the operation of nuclear reactors, the use and storage of explosives and the spraying of crops.

Note: The operation of an airplane is not considered to be an ultrahazardous activity, but some courts will rule that strict liability for ground damage from aviation accidents is applicable.

D.    Defenses

1. Contributory Negligence
Contributory negligence is not a defense unless the party knew of the abnormally dangerous activity.

2. Assumption of Risk
If the party unreasonably exposed itself to the risk, fully aware of its existence, the defendant will not be liable.

3. Comparative Negligence
Comparative negligence will be used to reduce damages.

## CASE CLIPS

### Marshall v. Ranne (1974) Ke
**Facts:**  Marshall's hand was severely injured by Ranne's vicious hog. Marshall knew of the hog's tendencies but failed to protect himself.
**Issue:**  Does contributory negligence bar recovery for damages in an action based on strict liability involving a vicious animal?
**Rule:**    The defense of contributory negligence is not available in strict liability actions for injuries caused by a vicious animal, unless the plaintiff's negligence directly allowed the animal to escape from the defendant's land.

### Fletcher v. Rylands Ke, Fr
**Facts:**  The defendant had a reservoir constructed close to the plaintiff's coal mines. When the reservoir filled, water broke through an abandoned mine shaft and flooded the plaintiff's mines. Though the contractors and engineers were negligent, the defendant was not personally negligent.
**Issue:**  May a person be liable for damages caused despite the use of due care?

**In the Exchequer (1865):**
**Rule:** Unless damages are immediate, there can be no trespass. Unless the act is unlawful, there can be no nuisance. Unless there is negligence, there can be no liability.
**In the Exchequer Chamber (1866):**
**Rule:** One who brings *anything* on land which is likely to do mischief if it escapes is strictly liable for damages which are the natural consequence of its escape.
**In the House of Lords (1868):**
**Rule:** One is strictly liable for damages resulting from the dangerous *non-natural* use of land.

### Shipley v. Fifty Associates (1870) Ke
**Facts:** The plaintiff was injured when ice and snow that had naturally accumulated on the defendant's roof slid off and hit her in the head.
**Issue:** Is one strictly liable for damages caused by one's property?
**Rule:** One is strictly liable for damages caused by one's property (i.e., one has a duty to use the property in such a way that others will not be harmed).

### Siegler v. Kuhlman (1973) Ke, Ep
**Facts:** The trailer of the Kuhlman's truck disengaged and spilled gasoline on the road. The plaintiff was killed when the gas caught fire. The reason for the trailer's disengagement was unknown.
**Issue:** Is a defendant liable for injuries proximately caused by an inherently dangerous activity despite an absence of negligence?
**Rule:** Inherently dangerous activities are subject to strict liability.

### Koos v. Roth (1982) Ke
**Facts:** The defendant, a commercial grass seed producer, regularly burned his field after the seed was harvested. Without any negligence on the defendant's part, the plaintiff's adjoining field caught fire.
**Issue:** Is a party who engages in an activity that is not inherently dangerous liable in the absence of negligence if the activity was conducted in an abnormal manner?
**Rule:** An individual who engages in an activity in a manner that creates an uncontrollable danger of serious harm beyond the ordinary risks associated with that activity is strictly liable.

### Chavez v. Southern Pacific Transportation Co. (1976) Ke

**Facts:** Eighteen boxcars loaded with government-owned bombs exploded while being transported by Southern Pacific Transportation.

**Issue:** Is a party strictly liable for damages that result from an ultrahazardous activity when the party is obligated by law to perform the activity?

**Rule:** Parties who engage in ultrahazardous activities are strictly liable for damages caused by those activities, regardless of whether the party was obligated by law to engage in the activity.

### Lubin v. Iowa City (1964) Ke

**Facts:** Iowa City's underground water main broke, flooding the basement of Lubin's store. As a matter of policy, Iowa City did not inspect its pipes for repairs until they broke.

**Issue:** Is a party strictly liable when it deliberately fails to maintain its property?

**Rule:** Strict liability may be imposed on a party who deliberately keeps property that was not inherently dangerous in an inherently dangerous manner.

### Bierman v. City of New York (1969) Ke

**Facts:** Bierman's home was damaged by a water main break. She was unable to show any negligence on the part of the defendant.

**Issue:** May the rule of strict liability be applied to achieve the social goal of spreading a risk among many persons?

**Rule:** Cost spreading is a valid social goal and a valid reason to apply strict liability.

### McLane v. Northwest Natural Gas Co. (1970) Ke

**Facts:** Gas leaked from the Northwest Natural's gas tanks and exploded despite extensive precautions taken to avoid an accident.

**Issue:** Is an activity considered ultrahazardous when the risk of an accident is small?

**Rule:** The principal factor determining if an activity is ultrahazardous is whether the activity creates an additional risk to others which cannot be alleviated, and which arises from the extraordinary, exceptional, or abnormal nature of the activity.

### Yukon Equipment, Inc. v. Fireman's
### Fund Insurance Co. (1978) Ke, Fr

**Facts:** Thieves broke into Yukon's explosives warehouse and blew it up to destroy evidence of their crime. Fireman's sued to recover the damage that occurred to adjoining property, claiming that Yukon was strictly liable.

**Issue:** Is the storage of explosives an ultrahazardous activity?

**Rule:** The storage of explosives is inherently ultrahazardous, regardless of the storage location.

### Maye v. Tappan (1863) Ep

**Facts:** Maye and Tappan owned adjacent gold mines. Tappan entered Maye's mine and removed gold, erroneously believing he was still on his own property.

**Issue:** Has a trespass occurred when a party believed it was on its own property?

**Rule:** The intent required for a trespass is the intent to do the physical act of the trespass, and not the intent to trespass.

### Baker v. Snell (1908) Ep

**Facts:** The defendant's dog, known to have a propensity to bite, bit the plaintiff after the defendant's servant mischievously let the dog loose.

**Issue:** Must negligence be shown to make an animal owner liable for injuries inflicted by the animal?

**Rule:** An owner of an animal that is known to be dangerous is strictly liable for the animal's actions, even if the immediate cause of damage is the act of a third party.

### Spano v. Perini Corp. (1969) Ep

**Facts:** Spano's garage was damaged by the blasting activities of the defendants.

**Issue:** Is one liable for damages resulting from dangerous activities without a showing of negligence?

**Rule:** A person engaged in activities which involve a substantial risk of harm no matter the degree of care exercised are strictly liable for damages caused, regardless of fault.

### Madsen v. East Jordan Irrigation Co. (1942) Ep
**Facts:** The defendant's blasting caused Madsen's minks to panic and kill their young.

**Issue:** Is one who is engaged in an ultrahazardous activity strictly liable for indirect damages?

**Rule:** Parties engaged in ultrahazardous activities are strictly liable for direct, but not indirect damages.

### Sullivan v. Dunham (1900) Fr
**Facts:** Sullivan was killed by fragments from a tree that the defendant was using dynamite to remove.

**Issue:** Must negligence be proven to recover for a trespass to the body resulting from a dangerous activity?

**Rule:** A person is strictly liable for trespass damages proximately caused by the person's involvement in a dangerous activity.

## I.    INTRODUCTION

### A.    Interest Protected
The interest protected by nuisance is one's use and enjoyment of one's property, whereas trespass only protects one's interest in the possession of property.

### B.    Intent Requirement
A party must be aware of the harmful effects of its conduct. However, reckless, negligent, or ultrahazardous interference with a party's use of its land might suffice to show intent. The two types of nuisance are public and private.

## II.    PUBLIC NUISANCE

An interference with a right that is common to the general public or community. The elements of a public nuisance are:

### A.    Substantial Harm
Nuisance requires a substantial harm. This is unlike trespass where nominal damages are awarded even if no harm is done.

### B.    Injury to the Public at Large

### C.    Personal Harm is Separate from Public
If an individual party wants to recover damages that it suffered from a public nuisance, it must show that it suffered a different kind of harm than the general public.

## III.    PRIVATE NUISANCE

A substantial and unreasonable interference with a party's use or enjoyment of its land. The elements of a private nuisance are:

A.    Possessory Interest
The plaintiff must have a possessory interest in the land, e.g., a person who stays at a friend's house cannot sue a factory that pollutes the friend's lawn. However, a tenant has a sufficient possessory interest.

B.    Substantial Interference

1.  A nominal injury is not enough; the plaintiff must be actually and substantially discomforted.

2.  Whether an interference is substantial is determined by its effect on an average person; an extrasensitive person will not recover.

C.    Unreasonable Interference

1.  In determining unreasonableness, a court will balance the harm to the plaintiff against the benefits of the defendant's conduct to the community.

2.  The Restatement (2d) suggests an alternative test, providing that plaintiffs should also be reimbursed if the harm to the plaintiff is substantial *or* the harm outweighs the utility of the interference to the defendant.

3.  Regardless of the test used, the court will consider such factors as the character of the neighborhood, land values and the nature of the parties.

IV.    REMEDIES

A plaintiff has three possible remedies against a nuisance:

Mnemonic: **AID**

A.    Abatement by Self-Help
A party is allowed to use reasonable force to cure the nuisance after the defendant refuses a request to do so.

B. Injunction

An injunction will only be granted if the party succeeds in proving that its injuries outweigh the community's benefits from the defendant's activity. If successful, the party can shut down the defendant's operations and stop the nuisance.

C. Damages

Damages may be awarded for past and future harm in the case of ongoing or permanent nuisances.

V. DEFENSES

Mnemonic: **CARGO**

A. Contributory Negligence

Contributory negligence only applies if the plaintiff claims that the defendant negligently created the nuisance.

Note: There are other ways to fulfill the intent requirement, i.e., intentional, reckless or ultrahazardous conduct.

B. Assumption of Risk

Assumption of risk applies if the defendant engaged in negligent or ultrahazardous conduct. If the plaintiff acted unreasonably despite knowledge of a nuisance, the plaintiff will be barred from recovery.

A variation of assumption of risk that the courts recognize is when the plaintiff "comes to the nuisance."

1. Old Rule

If the defendant came to an area before the plaintiff, the plaintiff was barred from recovery.

2. Restatement (2d)

Coming to the nuisance is only one factor to look at in the balancing test.

C.   Governmental Authority
Conformity to local zoning laws and regulations is persuasive, though not conclusive evidence that an activity is not a nuisance.

D.   Others are Liable
When several parties combine to produce a nuisance, each party is only liable for the portion of damages it actually caused.

## CASE CLIPS

### Atkinson v. Bernard, Inc. (1960) Ke

**Facts:** Homeowners living near a small airport brought an action to enjoin flights from flying over their property. They argued that the airplanes trespassed on their airspace, creating noise and vibrations which substantially interfered with the use and enjoyment of their property.

**Issue:** Is an action to enjoin airport operations properly brought under the theory of nuisance or trespass?

**Rule:** Suits to enjoin all or part of the operations of an airport should be brought under the theory of nuisance rather than trespass.

### Railroad Commission of Texas v. Manziel (1962) Ke

**Facts:** The plaintiff sued to prevent the defendants from injecting salt water in their well to improve oil yield. The plaintiff claimed that the salt water would seep underground onto his property.

**Issue:** Is the subsurface invasion of land a trespass?

**Rule:** The traditional rules concerning the surface invasion of land do not apply to subsurface invasions. Public policy must be considered when determining if a subsurface invasion is a trespass.

**Note:** The court's determination that no trespass occurred was based on the need to ensure adequate oil production.

### Martin v. Reynolds Metals Co. (1959) Ke, Fr

**Facts:** Chemicals spewed from Reynolds Metals Company's plant caused the poisoning of Martin's cattle.

**Issue:** Does air pollution give rise to an action in trespass or in nuisance?

**Rule:**　Damage caused by air pollutants entering one's property may be recovered in a suit based on trespass. There is no requirement that the invading object be seen.

### Whalen v. Union Bag & Paper Co. (1913) Ke

**Facts:**　Union Bag's pulp plant discharged pollutants into a stream which passed by Whalen's property.

**Issue:**　Can an injunction to prohibit a nuisance be denied merely because the defendant's loss will be greater than the plaintiff's benefit?

**Rule:**　An injunction should not be set aside merely because the abatement of the nuisance causes the defendant far greater loss than it benefit's the plaintiff.

### Boomer v. Atlantic Cement Co., Inc. (1970) Ke, Ep, Fr

**Facts:**　Dirt, smoke and vibrations emanating from the defendant's cement plant were a nuisance to the plant's neighbors.

**Issue:**　Can a monetary award be substituted for an injunction in a nuisance action?

**Rule:**　If the effects of an injunction are significantly more severe than the effects of a nuisance to the plaintiff, a court may grant an injunction conditioned on the payment of permanent damages to the plaintiff. This payment would compensate for the total present and future economic loss to the plaintiff's property caused by the defendant's operations.

### State, Department of Environmental Protection v. Ventron Corp. (1983) Ke

**Facts:**　The defendants operated a mercury processing plant which dumped untreated toxic waste underground, polluting state waterways.

**Issue:**　Is the storage of toxic waste an abnormally dangerous activity for which a landowner may be held strictly liable?

**Rule:**　Mercury and other toxic wastes are abnormally dangerous and their disposal is an abnormally dangerous activity. Consequently, landowners are strictly liable for harm caused by toxic wastes that are stored on their property.

### Jost v. Dairyland Power Cooperative (1970) Ke

**Facts:** Jost and other neighbors of a Dairyland coal plant brought a nuisance suit to recover monetary damages for damaged crops and loss in the market value of their farmlands.

**Issue:** May damages be awarded for the permanent loss in market value of land due to a continuing nuisance?

**Rule:** A landowner is entitled to compensation for damages caused by permanent and continuing nuisances. The value of the damages which may be awarded is reflected in the diminution of the market value of the landowner's property.

### Copart Industries Inc. v.
### Consolidated Edison Company of New York, Inc. (1977) Ke

**Facts:** Copart Industries lost its car servicing business when the cars it worked on became discolored and pitted as a result of noxious emissions from Consolidated Edison's adjoining power plant. Copart brought a nuisance action grounded in negligence.

**Issue:** What type of conduct creates nuisance liability?

**Rule:** A defendant may be liable for nuisance for either negligent or intentional conduct.

### Bamford v. Turnley (1862) Ke

**Facts:** The defendant built a kiln and began making bricks in a residential neighborhood. The plaintiff sued for nuisance.

**Issue:** May activity on one's own land which is not wantonly or maliciously conducted be enjoined where it causes a diminution of the enjoyment of a neighbor's land?

**Rule:** One may be enjoined from conducting activities only if the activities are not necessary for the common and ordinary use and occupation of land.

### Spur Industries, Inc. v.
### Del E. Webb Development Co. (1972) Ke

**Facts:** Del Webb developed a residential area near Spur's feedlot where more than 20,000 cattle produced more than a million pounds of wet manure per day. Del Webb sued for nuisance, seeking an injunction. In addition to Del Webb, the residents of Del Webb's development were harmed by the nuisance.

**Issue:** May a plaintiff who has "come to the nuisance" be granted an injunction to abate the nuisance?

**Rule:** A plaintiff who has "come to the nuisance" ordinarily would not be granted injunctive relief. However, if the nuisance adversely affects innocent third parties as a result of the plaintiff having come to the nuisance, injunctive relief will be granted, but the plaintiff will have to indemnify the defendant for having caused the need for an injunction.

### Morgan v. High Penn Oil Co. (1953) Ep

**Facts:** Morgan brought a private nuisance action against High Penn Oil, whose refinery emitted nauseating gases and odors.

**Issue:** If a party is conducting an otherwise lawful act, can there be a nuisance in the absence of negligence?

**Rule:** A nuisance "per se" (at law) is an act, occupation or structure which is a nuisance at all times and under any circumstance, regardless of location or surroundings. Nuisances "per accidens" (in fact) are those which become nuisances by reason of their location, or the manner in which they are constructed, maintained, or operated. A nuisance "per accidens" need not be the result of negligence; it may be either intentional or unintentional.

### Fontainebleau Hotel Corp. v. Forty-Five Twenty-Five, Inc. (1959) Ep

**Facts:** The Eden Roc Hotel brought a private nuisance action to prevent the Fontainebleau Hotel from building an addition to its Miami Beach hotel that would block air and sunlight from the Eden Roc. There was evidence to indicate that the actions of the Fontainebleau were motivated partly by malice.

**Issue:** Can landowners be enjoined from using their land in a manner injurious to their neighbors if there is evidence of malicious intentions?

**Rule:** Landowners may use their property in any reasonable and lawful manner, even if motivated by spite, so long as they do not thereby deprive the adjoining landowners of any right of enjoyment of their property which is recognized and protected by law.

**Note:** The law does not recognize a right to light and air; consequently, it is not a nuisance to block them.

### Rodgers v. Elliott (1888) Ep

**Facts:** The defendant refused to stop ringing a church bell after the plaintiff's physician advised him that the noise would cause the plaintiff to have convulsions. The plaintiff brought a nuisance action seeking an injunction.

**Issue:** Can one be liable in nuisance to an abnormally sensitive plaintiff?

**Rule:** The standard of whether an activity is a nuisance is judged by its effect on an average person, not its effect upon an ultrasensitive plaintiff.

### Ensign v. Walls (1948) Ep

**Facts:** Neighboring homeowners brought a nuisance action to close the defendant's dog kennel because of odors and noise emanating from it. The homeowners had moved to the neighborhood after the kennel was established.

**Issue:** Is a party liable for a nuisance if was conducting the offending activities before the plaintiffs acquired their property interests (i.e., the plaintiffs "came to the nuisance")?

**Rule:** A nuisance may be abated even though it predated the plaintiff's property interests. The defense of "coming to the nuisance" is not absolute. Public policy concerns over health and safety may override it.

### Anonymous (1535) Ep

**Facts:** The plaintiff brought a private nuisance action to prevent the defendant from continually blocking a public highway and preventing its use.

**Issue:** Can a private action in nuisance be brought to recover damages suffered by the general public?

**Rule:** A party may assert a private action in nuisance for public damages only if the party has suffered greater damages than ordinary members of the public.

### Union Oil Co. v. Oppen (1974) Ep

**Facts:** Commercial fishermen suffered economic losses when Union Oil negligently caused an oil spill.

**Issue:** Does a cause of action lie for loss of prospective income caused by a defendant's negligence?

**Rule:** Foreseeable losses of prospective income can be recovered in a negligence action.

**Note:** This rule exists in only a few jurisdictions.

# Chapter 13

## PRODUCTS LIABILITY

Products liability refers to the liability of a seller/manufacturer whose product causes damage to a buyer, user, or even a bystander because it was defectively made.

## I.    NEGLIGENCE

A plaintiff can use ordinary negligence principles to hold a manufacturer liable for a defective product. At one time there was a requirement that a plaintiff be in privity with the seller, but that was abolished in *MacPherson v. Buick Motor Co.* A plaintiff may recover for personal injury and property damages.

A.    Manufacturer's Duty of Care
Plaintiffs may bring negligence actions against manufacturers if the manufacturers fail to properly ensure that:

1. the products are designed in a reasonably safe way;

2. the manufacturing system is reasonably error-free;

3. the products are reasonably tested/inspected;

4. the products are packaged and shipped with reasonable safety;

5. the components used are reasonably competent.

B.    Retailer
It is very difficult to hold the retailer of a product liable under a negligence theory. Usually retailers do not have a duty to inspect the products they sell. However, a retailer who knows or should know that a product was unreasonably defective has a duty to warn.

C.  Bystanders
Bystanders may be able to sue a manufacturer if they can show that they were foreseeable plaintiffs.

## II.  WARRANTY

Where a manufacturer of a product is not negligent, a party may still recover damages from the seller if it can be shown that the seller of the product made representations or warranties as to the quality of the product which proved to be false, regardless of whether it was known to be false. This applies to both implied and express warranties.

A.  Express Warranty (UCC)
An express warranty is not limited by privity; it extends to all members of a class that a seller intended to reach with the warranty. However, a warranty does not extend to resale if the manufacturer did not expect the product to be resold.

An express warranty can be made in several ways:

1.  a seller describes the product in a certain way;

2.  a seller uses a sample or model to show clients; or

3.  there is a written statement or clause in a contract.

B.  Implied Warranty
A warranty may be implied, even absent an express one from the fact that goods are being offered for sale.

1.  Implied Warranty of Merchantability
All products that are packaged in labelled containers are assumed to be fit for the ordinary purpose for which they are intended. This warranty applies if:

a.  the seller is regularly engaged in the sale of the product;

b.  the product is food and drink; or

c. the warranty is implied by the act of a seller in offering to sell the product.

2. Implied Warranty of Fitness for a Particular Purpose
This warranty is breached only if a seller misrepresents to a buyer, even unintentionally, that a product is suitable for a specific use for which it is not suitable, and the buyer, relying on the misrepresentation, is injured.

3. Privity
There is no requirement of privity between a buyer and a seller. An implied warranty runs with a product to any buyer.

The courts allow other parties to sue by one of two legal fictions that create privity:

a. Horizontal Privity
Most states allow a warranty to extend to a buyer's family and guests.

For example, Rob buys a car from Buick and lets Susan, his sister, drive the car. Susan crashes because the brakes are defective. Susan can sue Buick for breach of the implied warranty of merchantability.

b. Vertical Privity
Vertical privity extends to any foreseeable people using the product.

C. Defenses

Mnemonic: **Defensive Types Consciously Avoid Liability**

1. **D**isclaimers

a. Express
If a manufacturer uses a disclaimer of merchantability, it must be both apparent and specific in order to defeat the warranties.

      b. Implied
         If a good is sold "as is," this is viewed as an implied disclaimer of warranties.

  2. Timeliness
     A buyer who fails to give timely notification of a defect is barred from recovery.

  3. Comparative Negligence
     Some jurisdictions allow comparative negligence.

  4. Assumption of Risk
     Use of goods that are known to be defective will relieve a seller of liability.

  5. Limitation of Liability
     A manufacturer can place limits on the extent it must replace and repair defective products. This is only acceptable for business goods, as opposed to consumer goods.

D.   Damages

  1. Personal Injury
     A plaintiff can recover for personal injuries regardless of whether the plaintiff was in privity with the seller.

  2. Property Damage
     A plaintiff not in privity with a seller will not recover for property damage in most states under an implied warranty, but will recover in most states under an express warranty.

  3. Intangible Harm

      a. Direct Purchasers
         For an intangible harm, a direct purchaser will recover:

         i.   The decreased value of the product due to the defect.

ii. Any consequential damages a defendant had reason to expect at the time of sale.

b. Users or Bystanders
Under an implied warranty the majority of the courts will deny recovery to a user or a bystander for an intangible harm. Under an express warranty they may recover for an intangible harm, but it is unlikely that they will be able to prove that the warranty existed.

E. Advantage of Warranty-Based Actions Over Tort-Based Actions

1. If a plaintiff suffered purely economic harm, it is not usually recoverable under strict liability.

2. The statute of limitations is longer for a warranty action than for a tort action.

3. A plaintiff who is in direct privity with a defendant has an easier case under a warranty action because it is relatively easy to establish a duty and a breach.

III. STRICT PRODUCTS LIABILITY

A manufacturer is strictly liable if it places a defective product in the market that causes injury to others. There are several policy reasons for holding a manufacturer of a defective product strictly liable.

A. Better Position
A manufacturer is in a better position to anticipate and avoid defects.

B. Loss Spreading
A manufacturer can better spread the costs by charging all its customers more and using the money to compensate a plaintiff.

C.    Encourage Research
      Holding manufacturers liable will give them the incentive to
      develop safer products.

D.    Difficulty of Proof
      It is almost impossible for a plaintiff to prove a defendant was
      at fault given the complex technologies and procedures of
      modern production.

E.    Reciprocal Risk
      The rationale that a manufacturer marketed the product and
      therefore should be held responsible.

IV.   TYPES OF DEFECTS

      There are three general types of product defects for which a
      manufacturer may be held strictly liable:

A.    Construction/Manufacturing Defects [Restatement 2d § 402(a)]
      A manufacturing defect involves a product that is normally safe,
      but because of a mistake or error was defectively constructed.

      1. A manufacturer is strictly liable when it sells a product in a
         defective condition that is unreasonably dangerous to a
         consumer or a consumer's property if:

         a. the seller is regularly engaged in the business of selling
            this product; and

         b. the product reaches the ultimate consumer without any
            substantial change in the condition in which it was sold.

      2. No privity is required between the manufacturer and the
         plaintiff. However, the manufacturer is not liable if the
         plaintiff used the product in an abnormal manner.

3. Generally, a plaintiff has to prove that:

   a. the defendant manufactured the product;

   b. the product was defective;
     Some courts require a plaintiff to show that it was unreasonably unsafe, i.e., dangerous beyond what ordinary users would expect. Others allow res ipsa loquitur to be used to infer defectiveness;

   c. the product was both the actual and proximate cause of the plaintiff's injury; and

   d. the defect existed at the time the product left the defendant's factory/control. Courts will usually allow an inference of this fact.

B.   **Design Defects**
Design defects involve products that are manufactured according to plan, but are defective because they were improperly planned.

1. Types of Design Defects

   a. Structural Defect
     There is a structural defect if the product is not as durable as a reasonable person would expect. There is no requirement of super durability, but the product must pass a reasonableness standard.

   b. Lack of Safety Features
     It is no excuse that a competitor's product also lacks safety features. However, courts may excuse a lack of safety features if the burden of installing them exceeds the potential loss.

   c. Suitability for Foreseeable Unintended Use
     A product does not have to be designed to be safe for every possible use, but some misuses of a product are

foreseeable, and a **manufacturer** must take reasonable precautions to protect against those misuses.

2. A Plaintiff's Burden Is To Prove:

  a. the design was defective and caused the plaintiff's injury;

  b. there was a practical, safer alternative design.

3. Cost-Benefit Analysis
Does the inherent risk of a defective design outweigh its benefits? Consider:

  a. the gravity of the inherent risk;

  b. the likelihood that danger will occur;

  c. the mechanical feasibility of a safer alternative design;

  d. the financial cost of an improved design;

  e. the obviousness of the dangers; and

  f. the public expectations of a danger.

Some courts will instead consider whether the product was as safe as a reasonable consumer would expect it to be when used for an intended or foreseeable unintended purpose.

4. Defenses

  a. The plaintiff used the product in an unforeseeable, unintended manner.

  b. The product did not cause the injuries.

  c. The plaintiff knew of the defective design, but ignored it.

        d. Comparative negligence: compare the defective design and the plaintiff's negligence to reduce the defendant's damage liability.

C. Unavoidably Unsafe Products
Almost like a subgroup of manufacturing defects, the products included in this category are incapable of being made safe for their intended and ordinary use.

If a product is unavoidably unsafe but its benefits exceed its costs, a manufacturer is relieved of liability if it properly prepares, tests and labels the product.

1. Manufacturers are negligent if they:

    a. knew or should have known of the product's inherent dangers had they exercised reasonable care given the technology at the time the product was sold; and

    b. fail to adequately warn all foreseeable users.

2. Obvious Dangers
There is no general duty to warn against obvious dangers or against misuse of a product.

3. Prescription Drugs
A manufacturer of prescription drugs only has to warn a physician, who can use personal discretion in deciding whether to warn users.

## CASE CLIPS

**MacPherson v. Buick Motor Co. (1916)** Ke, Ep, Fr
**Facts:** MacPherson was injured when his car's defective wheel broke into fragments. He had bought the car from a dealer who had bought it from Buick Motors, the manufacturer of the car. A reasonable safety inspection would have revealed the defect in the wheel.

**Issue:** Is a manufacturer liable to one who is not a direct purchaser?
**Rule:** Manufacturers of products that are "reasonably certain to place life and limb in peril when negligently made" owe a duty of reasonable care to all foreseeable users.

### Henningsen v. Bloomfield Motors Inc. (1960) Ke

**Facts:** Henningsen was injured when her car's defective steering gear caused it to crash. When Henningsen's husband bought the car he signed a standard waiver of all warranties against the defendants.
**Issue:** When is an express waiver limiting a manufacturer's liability under the implied warranty of merchantability valid?
**Rule:** A waiver is valid unless the court finds the two parties are in a position of gross inequality of bargaining power.

### Escola v. Coca Cola Bottling Co. (1944) Ke, Ep, Fr

**Facts:** The plaintiff was injured when a soft drink bottle exploded in her hand. She asserted an action based on res ipsa loquitur.
**Issue:** Must a manufacturer's negligence be proven in an action to recover damages caused by a defective product?
**Rule:** A manufacturer is strictly liable if the defect in its product caused the plaintiff's injuries, the defect was present when the product left the manufacturer's control, and the plaintiff did not unreasonably misuse the product.

### Elmore v. American Motors Corp. (1969) Ke

**Facts:** A defective drive shaft manufactured by the defendant fell off Elmore's car, injuring Elmore and killing another person.
**Issue:** Is a manufacturer strictly liable for damages caused to a bystander by its defective product?
**Rule:** Consumers and bystanders may recover for injuries proximately caused by a defective product; strict liability may not be restricted by privity of contract.

### Goldberg v. Kollsman Instrument Corp. (1963) Ke, Ep

**Facts:** Goldberg was killed in an airplane crash that was caused by the airplane's defective altimeter, which the defendants manufactured but did not assemble.
**Issue:** Is a manufacturer of a defective component part strictly liable for injuries to parties not in privity with the manufacturer?

**Rule:** A component manufacturer is not strictly liable to parties not in privity with it. However, an assembler or final manufacturer is strictly liable for injuries caused by its product if the component was negligently made when it left the party's control and the injured party was a reasonably foreseeable user.

### Heaton v. Ford Motor Co. (1967) Ke
**Facts:** Heaton's new pickup truck tipped over when the rivets in the wheel came apart after he drove over a six inch rock.
**Issue:** What standard is used to determine whether a manufacturer is liable for its defective product when the plaintiff has not shown the manufacturer to be negligent?
**Rule:** If a product deviates from the standard of performance that would be reasonably expected by users of the product, a manufacturer will be liable even if no evidence of negligence is presented.

### Henderson v. Ford Motor Co. (1974) Ke
**Facts:** Henderson's Ford automobile crashed when the negligently designed gas filter prevented her from reducing speed.
**Issue:** Is a manufacturer obligated to construct its product in the best possible way?
**Rule:** Manufacturers must produce their products so that they are not unreasonably unsafe. However, they are under no obligation to use the most durable design.

### Barker v. Lull Engineering Co. (1978) Ke, Ep, Fr
**Facts:** Barker was injured while operating the defendant's defectively designed high-lift loader.
**Issue:** When is the design of a product considered defective?
**Rule:** A product's design is considered defective if either the dangers inherent in the product's design outweigh the product's usefulness, or if the product was less safe than the ordinary consumer would expect when used in an intended or reasonably foreseeable manner.

### Hammond v. International Harvester Co. (1982) Ke
**Facts:** Hammond lost his life while operating heavy equipment that his employer had purchased from the defendant. At the employer's request, the defendant had removed a standard safety device that, if not removed, would most likely have prevented the accident.

**Issue:** Is a manufacturer strictly liable for a design defect when the design of the product was altered due to a purchaser's request?

**Rule:** If a manufacturer fails to provide a product with every element necessary to make it safe, the product's design is considered defective and the manufacturer is strictly liable. A request by a purchaser to alter the product's design does not relieve the manufacturer of liability.

### MacDonald v. Ortho Pharmaceutical Corp. (1985) Ke, Ep, Fr

**Facts:** MacDonald was injured when she took contraceptive pills prescribed by her doctor and manufactured by the defendant. The defendant had given a warning about the product's dangers to the prescribing doctor, but did not give one to the consumer directly.

**Issue:** Does a manufacturer of contraceptive pills have a duty to directly warn the user of the product's risks?

**Rule:** A manufacturer of contraceptive pills has a duty to warn the ultimate users of the dangers of its product.

**Note:** This is an exception to the general rule that manufacturers of prescription drugs need only warn the doctor of any dangers that exist.

### Crocker v. Winthrop Laboratories (1974) Ke

**Facts:** Crocker became addicted to a drug manufactured by Winthrop Laboratories that they represented as nonaddictive.

**Issue:** Are manufacturers liable for the breach of an express warranty they honestly believe to be true?

**Rule:** Manufacturers are liable for breaching an express warranty if it is found to be false even if they reasonably believed it to be true, and could not have possibly known that it was false.

### Beshada v. Johns-Manville Products Corp. (1982) Ke

**Facts:** The plaintiffs contracted lung disease from asbestos produced by the defendants. The defendants argued that they could not warn of its dangers because they were unknown at the time of marketing.

**Issue:** Can one who fails to warn of a product risk claim that the danger was undiscoverable at the time the product was marketed?

**Rule:** Strict liability is imposed on those who fail to warn of a product's risk despite the fact that the "state of scientific knowledge" at the time made discovery of these dangers impossible.

**Note:** This rejects the "state of the art" defense.

### Feldman v. Lederle Laboratories (1984) Ke, Fr
**Facts:** Feldman was not warned that the antibiotic she used would discolor her teeth. The manufacturer knew of the possibility of such side effects but did not provide warnings until four years later.
**Issue:** Is a manufacturer assumed to be aware of reasonably obtainable information about its product?
**Rule:** A manufacturer is generally assumed to know all reasonably obtainable general information about its product, but may avoid liability for an accident if it can prove that it lacked the information that would have prevented the accident.

### Findlay v. Copeland Lumber Co. (1973) Ke
**Facts:** Findlay was injured when he fell off the defendant's defectively manufactured ladder. Findlay was negligent in using the ladder.
**Issue:** Does contributory negligence defeat a products liability action based on strict liability?
**Rule:** Contributory negligence does not preclude recovery in a strict product liability action so long as the plaintiff did not assume the risk of the product defect.

### Micallef v. Miehle Co. (1976) Ke, Ep
**Facts:** Micallef was injured when he stuck his hand into a fast moving printing press to remove an object despite knowing of the danger. The machine had no safety guards to protect against such dangers.
**Issue:** Must a manufacturer install a safety device to protect users from an obvious danger?
**Rule:** A manufacturer is not relieved of its duty to protect users from an unreasonable danger because the danger is obvious.

### Daly v. General Motors Corp. (1978) Ke, Ep, Fr
**Facts:** Daly, intoxicated and not wearing his seat belt, was thrown from his car in an accident because of a defective door latch. He would not have been thrown from his car had he worn his seat belt.
**Issue:** Will a plaintiff's comparative negligence reduce a products liability damage award?
**Rule:** Damages in strict liability actions for defective products can be reduced by a plaintiff's failure to exercise reasonable care to the extent that the lack of care contributed to the plaintiff's injury.

### Price v. Shell Oil Co. (1970) Ke

**Facts:** Price was injured while working on a truck that his employer had leased from the defendant.

**Issue:** Are bailors and lessors of property strictly liable for injuries caused by their leased property?

**Rule:** The doctrine of strict liability in tort, already applicable to sellers of personal property, is also applicable to bailors and lessors of such property. The distributor of property is strictly liable regardless of who retains title to the property.

### Acosta v. Honda Motor Co., Ltd. (1983) Ke

**Facts:** Acosta was injured when the rear wheel of his motorcycle came loose. He was awarded punitive damages in a products liability suit.

**Issue:** Are punitive damages appropriate to products liability actions?

**Rule:** Where a plaintiff proves by clear and convincing evidence that the defendant's conduct was outrageous, punitive damages may be awarded in products liability actions.

### Grimshaw v. Ford Motor Co. (1981) Ke

**Facts:** Grimshaw was awarded punitive damages when her Ford Pinto burst into flames after being struck by another car. Ford was aware that its Pintos could not withstand high speed accidents, but failed to warn its consumers or remedy the problem.

**Issue:** Can punitive damages be awarded against a manufacturer for the defective design of its product?

**Rule:** Punitive damages may be awarded against companies that manufacture or mass produce products when evidence of malice in designing the product is presented.

### Winterbottom v. Wright (1842) Ep

**Facts:** Wright had a contract to supply and maintain mail coaches for the Postmaster General. Winterbottom's employer had a contract to supply the Postmaster with horses and drivers. Winterbottom, a driver, was injured when a coach broke.

**Issue:** Is one who contracts with a party liable to a third party injured by a breach of the contract?

**Rule:** One is not liable to third parties for negligently performing a private contract.

### McCabe v. Liggett Drug Co. (1953) Ep

**Facts:** The plaintiff was injured by an exploding coffee maker, which was purchased from the defendant.

**Issue:** Does an implied warranty of merchantability accompany a product when it is purchased?

**Rule:** When a product is purchased it is accompanied by an implied warranty that the product is reasonably suitable for its intended use.

### East River Steamship Corp. v. Transamerica Delaval (S.Ct. 1986) Ep, Fr

**Facts:** The plaintiff chartered a supertanker which suffered engine damage. They sued the manufacturer for the cost of engine repairs and for lost income while the ship was out of service.

**Issue:** Is a manufacturer of a commercial product liable in tort for damages to the product itself?

**Rule:** (Blackmun, J.) A manufacturer in a commercial relationship has no duty under either a negligence or strict products liability theory to prevent a product from injuring itself.

**Note:** A manufacturer may be liable, however, under contract law.

### Murphy v. E.R. Squibb & Sons, Inc. (1985) Ep

**Facts:** Murphy suffered injuries after taking a defective drug sold to her by the defendant, a pharmacist.

**Issue:** Are those who provide professional services strictly liable for alleged defects in products they sell?

**Rule:** Unlike sales retailers, those who provide professional services to their customers are not strictly liable for the products they sell that are related to the service they provide.

### Pouncey v. Ford Motor Co. (1972) Ep

**Facts:** Pouncey was injured when a blade flew off his car's radiator. At trial he used expert testimony to suggest that the blade flew off because of metal fatigue which was reasonably foreseeable.

**Issue:** May negligence in the construction of a product be inferred from circumstantial evidence?

**Rule:** A jury may use circumstantial evidence to infer a manufacturer's negligence in constructing a product.

### Volkswagen of America, Inc. v. Young (1974) Ep

**Facts:** The plaintiff was killed when his car's seat was separated from the car after the car was hit.

**Issue:** Must an automobile's design include precautions to prevent injuries in the event of an accident in order to fulfill the requirement that a product be fit for its "intended use?"

**Rule:** An automobile manufacturer is liable for a design defect which the manufacturer could have reasonably foreseen would cause or increase injuries upon impact, and which is not patent or obvious to the user.

### Cann v. Ford Motor Co. (1981) Ep

**Facts:** The plaintiffs were injured when their car shifted itself into reverse because of a design defect. Ford redesigned its cars to avoid such accidents in the future.

**Issue:** Can a plaintiff introduce evidence of a defendant's remedial measures subsequent to the accident as proof that the product was defectively designed?

**Rule:** Evidence of post-accident remedial repairs by a manufacturer are not admissible to prove the existence of a design defect.

### Brown v. Superior Court (Abbott Laboratories) (1988) Ep

**Facts:** The plaintiffs suffered injuries from taking a defective drug that prevented miscarriages.

**Issue:** Is a manufacturer of prescription drugs strictly liable for injuries resulting from design defects?

**Rule:** A drug manufacturer is not strictly liable for injuries from a prescription drug so long as the drug was properly prepared and it included warnings of any dangers that were either known or reasonably scientifically knowable at the time of distribution.

### Camacho v. Honda Motor Co., Ltd. (1987) Fr

**Facts:** Camacho's leg was injured after he was involved in a motorcycle accident. The motorcycle did not have crash bars which were available on other types of motorcycles at the time of its purchase.

**Issue:** Is the unreasonably dangerous and defective nature of a product's design determined by the ordinary consumer's contemplation of open and obvious danger?

**Rule:** The unreasonableness of a product's design is not determined by consumer expectation, but is primarily determined by technical, scientific information. Factors to be considered are (1) the usefulness of the product, (2) the safety of the product, (3) the availability of a safer alternative product of comparable utility, (4) the manufacturer's ability to make the product safer without effecting its utility, (5) the user's awareness of the product's inherently dangerous nature, and (6) the manufacturers ability to spread losses or to carry liability insurance.

### Hahn v. Sterling Drug, Inc. (1986) Fr
**Facts:** Hahn's daughter was seriously injured after ingesting an "over-the-counter topical analgesic" manufactured by Sterling Drug. The trial court granted a directed verdict to Sterling concerning the adequacy of the warnings provided.
**Issue:** May a court direct a verdict concerning the adequacy of a manufacturer's warning?
**Rule:** The adequacy of a manufacturer's warning is a question of fact and must be submitted to a jury.

### Huber v. Niagara Machine and Tool Works (1988) Fr
**Facts:** Huber's hand got caught in a mechanical power press when his foot slipped and hit a foot-operated starter switch that had its safety devices removed. The foot switch had been manufactured and sold with the safety devices.
**Issue:** Does a manufacturer have a duty to warn users about dangers related to the misuse and modification of its products?
**Rule:** If a product is safe when sold, the manufacturer does not have to warn about the dangers related to the product's misuse or modification, unless such misuse or modification is foreseeable.

### White v. Wyeth Laboratories, Inc. (1988) Fr
**Facts:** White, an infant, suffered permanent brain damage after being injected with a DPT vaccine manufactured by Wyeth Laboratories.
**Issue 1:** Are all prescription drugs considered "unavoidably unsafe" such that their manufacturers are immune from strict liability conditioned on the proper preparation of the drug and the proper provision of directions and warnings?

**Rule 1:** Prescription drugs, vaccines, or like products are not "unavoidably unsafe" per se; they are only "unavoidably unsafe" if no alternative design exists which effectively accomplishes the same purpose with less risk.

**Issue 2:** What constitutes adequate warning for an "unavoidably unsafe" product?

**Rule 2:** A manufacturer of an unavoidably unsafe prescription drug provides adequate warning when it reasonably discloses all risks inherent in the use of the drug of which the manufacturer, being held to the standard of an expert in the field, knew or should have known to exist.

**Note:** The qualified immunity from strict liability for manufacturers of "unavoidably unsafe" products is given in Restatement (2d) § 402A, Comment *k*.

### Hoven v. Kelble (1977) Fr

**Facts:** The plaintiff suffered a heart attack while undergoing a lung biopsy by the defendant.

**Issue:** Does the doctrine of strict products liability apply to improper medical care?

**Rule:** The doctrine of strict products liability does not apply to medical services.

### Hauter v. Zogarts (1975) Fr

**Facts:** Hauter was injured by a golf practice set that advertised that the "completely safe ball will not hit player." The manufacturer argued that it was understood that no device could protect a person from the normal hazards of golf.

**Issue:** Can a manufacturer modify an implied or express warranty?

**Rule:** A manufacturer's attempts to modify an implied or express warranty will not be effective unless the manufacturer can prove that the disclaimer was clear to all relevant parties.

# Chapter 14

## ALTERNATIVE COMPENSATION SYSTEMS

## I.   EMPLOYMENT INJURIES

Worker's compensation does not bar an intentional tort action since harm from an intentional tort is not a risk inherent in the workplace.

A negligent party can obtain limited contribution from a comparatively negligent employer in an amount proportional to the employer's percentage of negligence, but not to exceed the employer's total worker's compensation liability to the employee.

## II.   AUTOMOBILE ACCIDENT INJURIES

No-fault laws, which compensate victims of automobile accidents without regard to fault, are constitutional because they serve the public policy objectives of speedy adjudication and elimination of unnecessary cases from the judicial system.

## CASE CLIPS

**Sindell v. Abbott Laboratories (1980)** Ke
**Facts:**  Sindell alleged that she suffered injuries from a drug manufactured by the defendants and approximately 195 other companies.
**Issue:**  When several manufacturers distribute the same product, how should liability for damages caused by the product be apportioned?
**Rule:**  When several manufacturers produce identical products which injure a plaintiff, and it is impossible to know which manufacturer produced the specific product that caused the injury, the liability of the defendants is proportionate to their share of the overall market. To avoid such liability, a manufacturer would have to prove its product did not cause plaintiff's injuries.

### Ayers v. Township of Jackson (1987) Ke

**Facts:**  By its operation of a landfill, Jackson Township contaminated its residents' well water. The township was found liable under the New Jersey Tort Claims Act.

**Issue:**  What proof is needed to justify compensation for medical surveillance under the Tort Claims Act?

**Rule:**  The cost of medical surveillance is compensable when expert testimony proves the toxicity of the chemicals, the seriousness of the diseases at risk and the value of early diagnosis through reasonable and necessary surveillance.

### Wright v. Central Du Page Hospital Association (1976) Ke

**Facts:**  The plaintiff challenged the constitutionality of a statutory provision limiting medical malpractice judgments to $500,000.

**Issue:**  May recovery for a specific type of tort be limited by statute?

**Rule:**  Statutorily limiting recovery for a specific type of tort, such as medical malpractice actions, is arbitrary and unconstitutional.

### Johnson v. St. Vincent Hospital, Inc. (1980) Ke

**Facts:**  The plaintiff challenged the constitutionality of a statute that required malpractice claims to be submitted to a review panel and set limitations on the damages that could be recovered.

**Issue:**  May a state require malpractice claims to be submitted to a panel and place limitations on the damages that may be recovered?

**Rule:**  A requirement to submit medical malpractice claims to a review panel does not violate the right of trial by jury and access to the courts. Furthermore, a state may have a legitimate regulatory interest in limiting the damages that may be recovered.

### Kane v. Johns-Manville Corp. (1988) Ke

**Facts:**  As a result of present and expected suits, the defendant filed a voluntary petition in bankruptcy under Chapter 11. Kane, on behalf of himself and future third parties challenged the Bankruptcy Court's confirmation of the Plan of Reorganization.

**Issue:**  Does an injured plaintiff have standing to assert the rights of future claimants by challenging a reorganization plan?

**Rule:**  An injured plaintiff lacks sufficient standing to challenge a reorganization plan on the grounds that the plan would violate the rights of future claimants and other third parties.

### Ives v. South Buffalo Railway Co. (1911) Ke

**Facts:** Under the worker's compensation laws, the plaintiff, a railroad employee, was entitled to damages caused by a necessary risk of his employment regardless of fault.

**Issue:** Are worker's compensation statutes that make an employer liable regardless of fault constitutional?

**Rule:** No-fault worker's compensation statutes violate an employer's right to due process and, therefore, are unconstitutional.

### New York Central Railroad Co. v. White (S.Ct. 1917) Ke

**Facts:** White sought to recover for damages against the defendant under New York's worker's compensation statute.

**Issue:** Is a worker's compensation statute constitutional?

**Rule:** (Pitney, J.) A worker's compensation statute is a valid expression of the government's right to legislate rules concerning the public interest, and thus is constitutional.

### Whetro v. Awkerman (1970) Ke

**Facts:** Whetro was injured when a tornado destroyed his place of employment. His employers claimed no liability because the tornado was an "Act of God," as opposed to a work related hazard.

**Issue:** Are injuries resulting from "Acts of God" during the course of employment compensable under the Worker's Compensation Act?

**Rule:** It is no longer necessary to establish a relationship of proximate causality between employment and an injury to establish compensability under the Worker's Compensation Act. It is not a defense that the injury was caused by an "Act of God."

### Beauchamp v. Dow Chemical Co. (1986) Ke, Ep

**Facts:** Beauchamp brought an action against his employer alleging that the injury he suffered at his workplace was intentional.

**Issue:** Under what circumstances is a workplace injury considered to be an intentional tort by the employer?

**Rule:** Where an employer intended an act that injured an employee and knew that the injury was substantially certain to occur from the act, the employer has committed an intentional tort against its employee.

### Lambertson v. Cincinnati Corp. (1977) Ke

**Facts:** Lambertson was injured by a press brake that his employer, Hutchinson Manufacturing, purchased from Cincinnati Corp. The jury found that all three parties were negligent.

**Issue:** How are comparative negligence and worker's compensation statutes reconciled?

**Rule:** A negligent third party can obtain limited contribution from a comparatively negligent employer in an amount proportional to the employer's percentage of negligence, but not to exceed the employer's total worker's compensation liability to the employee.

### Hammontree v. Jenner (1971) Ke

**Facts:** Jenner had a past history of epileptic seizures. After 14 years without a seizure, one occurred causing him to have a car accident in which Hammontree was injured. Jenner had a valid driver's license and the authorities knew of his condition.

**Issue:** Is there strict liability for accidents occurring due to sudden forces beyond a defendant's control?

**Rule:** An accident caused by a force outside one's control will not lead to liability. However, if the person knew or should have known that the uncontrollable force was likely to come on suddenly, the person's conduct may be negligent.

### Pinnick v. Cleary (1971) Ke, Ep

**Facts:** The plaintiff was involved in a car accident and was barred from recovery for mental pain and suffering because he did not meet the requirements of the state no-fault insurance law. He would not have been barred under common law.

**Issue:** Is a statute that places constraints on the availability of relief for pain and suffering unconstitutional?

**Rule:** A government has a legitimate interest in speedy adjudication and lessening the burden of litigation in its courts. Legislation that sets objective criteria to avoid speculative and exaggerated claims is constitutional.

### Shavers v. Kelly (1978) Ke

**Facts:** The plaintiff challenged the constitutionality of Michigan's No-Fault Insurance Act because it partially abolished the common law recovery for negligently caused accidents.

**Issue:** Does a No-Fault Act violate due process by partially abolishing a tort remedy for persons injured by the negligence of others?
**Rule:** The abolition of a tort remedy for injuries is constitutional if it bears a reasonable relationship to a permissible legislative objective.

### Usery v. Turner Elkhorn Mining Co. (S.Ct. 1976) Ke

**Facts:** Turner Elkhorn Mining challenged the constitutionality of a federal statute that provided benefits for miners suffering from Black Lung disease by creating several presumptions in their favor (e.g., any miner with 10 years of experience who died from a respiratory disease is rebuttably presumed to have died from Black Lung disease).
**Issue:** Is a statute that creates presumptions unconstitutional?
**Rule:** (Marshall, J.) A statute is not unconstitutional for enacting presumptions if Congress did not act in an arbitrary or irrational manner.

### Duke Power Co. v. Carolina Environmental Study Group (S.Ct. 1978) Ke

**Facts:** The plaintiffs challenged the constitutionality of the Price-Anderson Act, which limited the total liability for a nuclear disaster.
**Issue:** Can Congress impose a limitation on liability for an activity that is licensed by the federal government?
**Rule:** (Burger, C.J.) Limiting liability is an acceptable method for Congress to utilize in encouraging the private development of certain activities.

### Industrial Union Department v. American Petroleum Institute (S.Ct. 1980) Ke

**Facts:** American Petroleum challenged the government's regulations regarding the use of the chemical benzene. The government enacted these strict regulations to limit employees' exposure to benzene.
**Issue:** Can the federal government place stringent technological and economic limitations on chemical exposure?
**Rule:** (Stevens, J.) A clearly significant risk of material health impairment must be shown before the federal government can impose the strictest controls on a chemical.

## American Textile Manufacturers Institute v. Donovan (S.Ct. 1981) Ke

**Facts:** The plaintiffs challenged the validity of federal standards that limited occupational exposure to cotton dust claiming that the cost of the standards exceeded their benefits.

**Issue:** Must safety regulations be justified by a cost-benefit analysis?

**Rule:** (Brennan, J.) The federal government is not required to establish that the costs of a health related safety regulation bear any reasonable relationship to its benefits. A feasibility analysis is required as opposed to a cost-benefit analysis.

## Matter of Richardson v. Fielder (1986) Ep

**Facts:** Richardson was killed while he was engaged in a theft at his workplace during working hours.

**Issue:** Are worker's compensation benefits awarded for injuries caused by an employee's non-work related illegal activities that occur during the course of employment?

**Rule:** Worker's compensation benefits can be awarded where an injury to an employee results from an illegal activity during the course of employment when the employer knows about and tolerates the illegal activity.

## Wilson v. Workers' Compensation Appeals Board (1976) Ep

**Facts:** The plaintiff, a teacher, was injured while driving to school.

**Issue:** Are worker's compensation benefits awarded for injuries incurred while commuting?

**Rule:** Worker's compensation benefits are not awarded for injuries sustained while commuting.

## Dowdy v. Motorland Insurance Co. (1980) Ep

**Facts:** Dowdy was injured by a bundle of steel that fell off a loading dock as he prepared to unload his truck. The defendants claimed that Dowdy could not recover damages under no-fault insurance because he was not injured while using a vehicle, as his policy required.

**Issue:** Does an accident involving a parked car fall within the requirements of no-fault statute?

**Rule:** No-fault insurance law can be invoked for an accident involving a parked vehicle only if the vehicle was parked in a way that caused an unreasonable risk, the injury was due to equipment permanently mounted on the vehicle, or the injury was sustained by a person who was occupying or entering the vehicle.

# Chapter 15

## MISREPRESENTATION

### I.  INTRODUCTION

This chapter addresses the tort of misrepresentation individually and does not discuss it as an element of another tort, which it may sometimes be. Generally, misrepresentation involves false statements that cause pecuniary harm. It usually occurs when two parties enter into a contract where one party is hiding or misstating an important fact that would affect the other party's willingness to enter into the contract.

### II.  CONCEALMENT AND NONDISCLOSURE

A.  Concealment
Concealment involves misstating or hiding the truth through words or actions.

It must relate to a material element of the agreement between the parties. Materiality is generally determined by what a reasonable person would consider material. However, if the defendant actually knows that some issue is extremely important to the plaintiff, then that issue is material.

B.  Nondisclosure
Nondisclosure occurs in situations where a party withholds information, as opposed to taking an affirmative step such as lying. A party is liable for nondisclosure if:

1.  There is a fiduciary relationship, e.g., attorney-client;

2.  The party withholds new information that makes a previously made statement false; or

3.  The nondisclosing party knows that the other party is mistaken about an essential and material fact.

C.  Intent

1.  Intent to Misrepresent
    The intent to misrepresent exists if the party:

    a.  Made the statement knowing or believing it to be false.

    b.  Implied or stated that the party had greater confidence in the accuracy of its statement than it actually did.

    c.  Implied or stated that the statement was based on more solid grounds than it actually was.

2.  Intent to Induce Reliance
    A party's intent to cause a plaintiff to rely on its misrepresentations can be extended to remote persons if the party acts in a way to induce their reliance.

III.  BASIS OF LIABILITY

A.  Third Parties
    A party who makes a negligent misstatement is only liable to the limited group of persons it intends to reach or that it knows its recipients intend to reach.

B.  Business
    Liability is most often allowed in business relationships.

C.  Strict Liability
    One may not be strictly liable for a misrepresentation unless:

    1.  The misrepresentation is made in a sale, rental or exchange transaction. There must be privity for liability to exist.

    2.  The misrepresentation is made by a seller of chattels.

## IV. RELIANCE AND OPINION

In order to recover for misrepresentation, a plaintiff must prove that the reliance on the misstatement was justified.

A. Statements of Fact v. Opinions

Reliance on a misrepresentation as to a fact is almost always justified, unless the relied upon representation is obviously false. Reliance on a false statement of opinion is only justified if:

1. the defendant has worked to gain the plaintiff's trust;

2. the defendant is or presents himself to be an expert; or

3. a fiduciary relationship exists between the parties.

B. Puffing

Salespersons are allowed to engage in some puffing as part of their sales pitch even if they somewhat exaggerate the product's attributes.

## V. LAW

Historically, statements of law were considered to be opinions. However, the modern trend is to handle statements of law in the same manner as all other statements.

## VI. PREDICTION AND INTENTION

A false prediction of future events is considered a statement of opinion, but a false representation of a person's intentions is a statement of fact.

## VII. DAMAGES

A plaintiff can recover any damages that were proximately caused by a defendant's misrepresentation. A plaintiff can recover consequential damages, as well as reliance damages, but not nominal damages.

A.   Reliance
     Reliance damages are damages directly incurred because of reliance on a negligent misrepresentation.

B.   Consequential
     Consequential damages are damages that indirectly result from reliance on a misrepresentation. A party can recover these damages only if they can be proved with sufficient certainty.

## CASE CLIPS

### Chandelor v. Lopus (1603) Ke

**Facts:** The defendant, a goldsmith, sold a gem to the plaintiff after misrepresenting the quality of the stone.

**Issue:** Is a sale of falsely represented goods actionable as deceit?

**Rule:** False representation of goods by a seller is not actionable unless the seller made a warranty at the time of sale.

### Pasley v. Freeman (1789) Ke, Ep

**Facts:** Freeman lied about a third party's financial status, persuading Pasley to do business with the third party. Freeman did not receive any monetary benefit from his deceit.

**Issue:** May an action for deceit be asserted against a party who makes false statements for no pecuniary gain?

**Rule:** An action for deceit can be asserted by one who is injured by the false representations of another even if the false statements were not made for contractual or pecuniary advantage.

### Price-Orem Investment Company v.
### Rollins, Brown and Gunnell, Inc. (1986) Ke

**Facts:** The defendant was hired by a general contractor to survey a site owned by the plaintiff. The defendant erred in certifying the property's boundaries, and the plaintiff consequently lost money.

**Issue:** Is a party liable for damages incurred by another who reasonably and foreseeably relies upon the party's negligent misrepresentations, despite a lack of privity between the parties?

**Rule:** Under the tort of negligent misrepresentation, a party injured by reasonable reliance upon another's careless or negligent misrepresentation of a material fact may recover damages resulting from that injury when the party who made the misrepresentation had a pecuniary interest in the transaction, was in a superior position to know the material facts, and should have reasonably foreseen that the injured party was likely to rely upon the representation.

### Johnson v. Davis (1985) Ke

**Facts:** Johnson knew, but failed to disclose, that there had been problems with the roof of his home, which Davis purchased. In fact, Johnson assured Davis that a prior problem with the roof was minor and had been corrected.

**Issue 1:** Must a seller of realty disclose latent material defects to a buyer?

**Rule 1:** Where the seller of a home, new or used, knows of facts materially affecting the value of the property which are not readily observable or known to the buyer, the seller is under a duty to disclose them to the buyer.

**Issue 2:** Is a seller who affirmatively misrepresents a material fact liable?

**Rule 2:** A seller is liable for fraudulent misrepresentation if the seller makes a false statement concerning a material fact, intends that the representation induce another to act on it, and a consequent injury by the party acting in reliance on the representation occurs.

### Watson v. Avon Street Business Center, Inc. (1984) Ke

**Facts:** The plaintiff bought a warehouse with a leaky roof. Prior to the purchase, the plaintiff inspected the roof. The seller's agent told the plaintiff it was "a good roof."

**Issue:** May a buyer who partially investigates the condition of that which is to be bought later maintain a suit for fraud in the inducement?

**Rule:** A buyer who is directed to sources of information and who personally begins an examination of the facts is charged with all the knowledge which would have been obtained had the examination been conducted diligently and completely. Consequently, the buyer cannot complain about a misleading seller's representation since reliance on the representation would be unreasonable.

### Vulcan Metals Co. v. Simmons Mfg. Co. (1918) Ke, Ep

**Facts:** Vulcan Metals sued the defendants for misrepresentations they made about the "absolutely perfect" condition of their machinery.

**Issue:** When are false statements made by a seller about a product considered an opinion (i.e., not actionable as misrepresentation)?

**Rule:** When a buyer and a seller have an equal bargaining position (e.g., a buyer has ample opportunity to examine a product), a false opinion is considered non-actionable "puffing."

### Stark v. Equitable Life Assurance Society (1939) Ke

**Facts:** Stark bought an insurance policy from the defendants that provided him a lawyer free of charge in the event of accident or injury. After an accident, Stark was incorrectly told by one of the defendant's agents that he could not recover.

**Issue:** Is a party who agrees to advise another on a matter of law obligated to act honestly and with due care?

**Rule:** Although misrepresentations of the law are ordinarily not actionable, when parties volunteer such information they are liable for misrepresentation if they do not give honest and fair advice.

### Burr v. Board of County Commissioners
### of Stark County (1986) Ke

**Facts:** The defendant represented to Burr that a child offered to Burr for adoption was healthy, had a healthy mother and was born in a city hospital. In fact, the defendant knew the child was born in a mental institution to mentally retarded parents and had inherited mental deficiencies.

**Issue:** Does the doctrine of sovereign immunity preclude a suit for fraud against a political subdivision?

**Rule:** If a plaintiff proves each element of fraud, the doctrine of sovereign immunity will not shield a political subdivision from responsibility for the fraudulent acts and misrepresentations of its employees and agents made in the performance of their services.

### Derry v. Peek (1889) Ke

**Facts:** The defendants issued a prospectus that said their railroad was approved by a Special Act of Parliament. Peek made investments based on the prospectus, but the company went bankrupt when it failed to obtain approval from the Board of Trade, as required.

**Issue:** Is an honest but false representation actionable as deceit?
**Rule:** The tort of deceit is not applicable when a false statement is made by one who honestly and reasonably believes in its truth.
**Note:** Under modern law, deceit would be found against a party who makes a statement with no reasonable basis to support it.

### Aldrich v. Scribner (1908) Ke

**Facts:** The defendant misrepresented that a plot of land he sold to the plaintiff contained 175 fruit trees. The defendant honestly believed this to be true.
**Issue:** Is a party strictly liable for false statements, or must the party act with knowledge that the statements are false or with reckless disregard for the truth to be liable?
**Rule:** A seller of land is strictly liable for untruthful statements that a buyer relies on, even if the seller honestly believed the statements to be true.
**Note:** This is the majority rule.

### Christenson v. Commonwealth Land Title Insurance Company (1983) Ke

**Facts:** Christenson sued to recover damages caused by the defendant's negligent acknowledgment of a document that incorrectly indicated that certain properties were available as security to Christenson. The plaintiff and defendant were not in privity of contract.
**Issue:** Absent privity of contract, may one who negligently makes a false statement be held liable?
**Rule:** A party with a pecuniary interest in a transaction and in a superior position to know material facts may be held liable for negligent misrepresentation, even in the absence of privity, if the party carelessly or negligently makes a false representation expecting another party to act in reliance thereon, and the other party reasonably does so, suffering a loss.

### Peek v. Gurney (1873) Ke

**Facts:** Peek sued a company's board of directors for misrepresentation and concealment of facts after he relied on their prospectus, which falsely described the company's strong financial position, to buy stock from another stockholder. The prospectus was targeted at buyer's of the first stock issue only.

**Issue:** Is one liable in misrepresentation for statements which are relied on by a party to its detriment if the representations were targeted to a class of persons to which the plaintiff was not a member.
**Rule:** A party is only liable to persons it intended to influence with misrepresentations even though other persons may have also been influenced.
**Note:** The modern view extends liability for intentional misrepresentation to all foreseeable plaintiffs.

### Credit Alliance Corporation v.
### Arthur Andersen & Co. (1985) Ke

**Facts:** The plaintiff, a credit company, relied on the defendant's erroneous financial analysis of a private company.
**Issue:** Absent privity of contract, is an accountant liable to a party that relies to its detriment upon a negligently prepared report?
**Rules:** An accountant is liable to a third party for a negligently prepared report if it was known the reports were to be used for a particular purpose.

### Williams v. Polgar (1974) Ke

**Facts:** Williams bought property from Polgar in reliance on a faulty abstract of title produced for Polgar. Williams sued the title company for negligent misrepresentation when he discovered the defective nature of the abstract.
**Issue:** Is a title company liable to persons it should have foreseen would rely on its title abstract if there is no contractual privity?
**Rule:** A negligent title company is liable to persons it should have foreseen would rely on its abstracts, as well as those it knew would rely on its abstracts, even if there is no contractual privity.

### Lucas v. Hamm (1961) Ke

**Facts:** Hamm, an attorney, prepared an invalid will. Lucas, an intended beneficiary of the will, sued Hamm for malpractice.
**Issue:** Is an attorney liable to a party that has suffered damages because of the attorney's improper work, though they were not in privity?
**Rule:** Third party beneficiaries who are not in privity with a lawyer may recover for the lawyer's negligence if they belong to a limited, foreseeable class of persons.

### Bishop v. E.A. Strout Realty Agency (1950) Ke

**Facts:** Bishop bought a tract of land for the purpose of opening a campsite. The defendant realty agency misrepresented to Bishop that the nearby lake was deep enough for camp activities. Bishop did not check the depth of the lake.

**Issue:** Is a seller's misrepresentation excused by a buyer's failure to examine the property purchased?

**Rule:** A buyer is not precluded from recovery for relying on a seller's misrepresentations of a matter that is not apparent to ordinary observation.

**Note:** This illustrates the general rule that a buyer has no duty to investigate before purchase.

### Turnbull v. LaRose (1985) Ke

**Facts:** Prior to consummation of a business transaction, LaRose, a seller, made certain assurances to the plaintiff, a buyer.

**Issue:** Does an action for misrepresentation lie where a buyer alleges reliance on a seller's opinions, as distinguished from statements of fact?

**Rule:** A seller's assurances, as distinguished from mere puffing, may be justifiably relied on by a buyer, and thus an action for misrepresentation would lie.

### Leyendecker & Associates, Inc. v. Wechter (1984) Ke

**Facts:** The defendant represented to Wechter that a lot which Wechter subsequently purchased contained 5,800 square feet. In fact, the lot was only 3389 square feet.

**Issue:** When a jury finds that there was no difference in the value of property as represented and as received, is a plaintiff precluded from recovering damages?

**Rule:** Absent a showing of a difference between the value represented and received, a plaintiff may not recover the benefit of the bargain, but may nonetheless recover any actual injuries.

### Edgington v. Fitzmaurice (1885) Ep

**Facts:** The plaintiff invested in the defendant's company, relying on defendant's prospectus that stated the money would be used for new investment. The money was actually used to pay off the company's debts.

**Issue:** What are the elements of an action for deceit/fraud?

**Rule:** To prove deceit, the plaintiff must show that the defendant knowingly or recklessly made a false statement with the intention that the plaintiff rely on the statement, and that the plaintiff acted in reliance, suffering some damages.

### Swinton v. Whitinsville Savings Bank (1942) Ep

**Facts:** Whitinsville Savings Bank did not disclose that the house it sold Swinton was infested with termites.

**Issue:** Must one disclose material facts if not asked to do so?

**Rule:** One is not liable for the failure to disclose information that is not requested.

**Note:** This rule has numerous exceptions.

### Laidlaw v. Organ (S.Ct. 1817) Ep

**Facts:** Organ contracted to buy tobacco from Laidlaw when Organ received information that its price would soon be going up. Laidlaw asked Organ if he had any information about the future price of tobacco, but Organ did not answer.

**Issue:** Must a buyer divulge external information about the price of a commodity about to be purchased?

**Rule:** (Marshall, C.J.) A buyer is under no obligation to divulge information that would affect the price of the commodity about to be purchased.

### Selman v. Shirley (1939) Ep

**Facts:** Shirley intentionally misrepresented the quantity of wood on the land that he sold to the plaintiffs.

**Issue:** Can a party that is defrauded by misrepresentation recover "the benefit of the bargain?"

**Rule:** A party that is defrauded by misrepresentation is entitled to recover "the benefit of the bargain" that would have been received.

**Note:** Benefit of the bargain damages are the difference between what a plaintiff actually paid for the property and what the property is worth.

### Ultramares Corporation v. Touche (1931) Ep

**Facts:** The plaintiff was injured when it loaned a third party money based on an erroneous report from the defendant, an accounting firm.

**Issue:** Is an accountant liable for negligent misrepresentation to a party where there is no privity of contract?

**Rule:** An accountant does not owe a duty of care to every party that uses financial statements it prepared and is not liable for errors in such statements unless those errors were intentionally fraudulent.

**Note:** The rule stated here does not represent the modern view.

## Chapter 16

### DEFAMATION

## I. NATURE OF A DEFAMATORY COMMUNICATION

The tort of defamation attempts to protect a person's reputation and relationships with others by making another liable who ridicules, vilifies or humiliates a person in the eyes of the public by use of an oral or written communication.

## II. LIBEL AND SLANDER

Mnemonic: **Libel is Letter**
**Slander is Spoken**

A. Libel
A recorded defamatory statement: written, recorded, computer tape, photograph, movie, etc.

1. Radio and TV

   a. Written Script
   All courts will consider defamatory remarks made on TV or radio to be libel if they are read off a prepared script.

   b. Ad Lib
   If defamatory remarks are not read from a script, the courts are split between whether it is libel or slander.

2. Damages
   General damages are presumed from libel; a plaintiff does not have to prove special damages unless the libel concerns an issue of public importance. See Ch. 16, VI, A.

B.  Slander
A spoken defamatory statement.

1. Damages
A plaintiff is generally required to prove special damages.
See Ch. 16, VI, B.

2. Slander Per Se
An exception to damages rule for slander is that damages will
be presumed if the slander involves one of these topics:

Mnemonic: **CAB RIDE**

a. Criminal Act
If it is implied that a plaintiff has committed a crime.

b. Business Reputation
If a plaintiff's professional reputation has been slandered.

c. Impurity
If a defendant implies that a woman is unchaste.

d. Disease Exposed
If a defendant implies that a plaintiff has a disease.

III.  PUBLICATION

Publication occurs when a defamatory statement is conveyed and
understood by a third person.

A.  Repetition
Each repetition of a defamatory statement creates a new cause
of action for defamation.

Exception:  Single Publication Rule
An entire edition of a book, newspaper or magazine is treated
as one publication even though the defamatory statement is
repeated numerous times. The time of publication occurs when
the product is first offered for sale.

B.  Republisher
    Each person who either says or repeats a defamatory statement is liable for defamation.

C.  Understanding
    For a publication to occur, the third party who receives it must understand it in its defamatory context.

    For example, if Susan makes a defamatory statement to Rob, who does not understand English, there is no publication. However, if Brett overhears and understands Susan, then a publication has occurred.

IV.  BASIS OF LIABILITY

For libel or slander to occur the following elements must exist:

Mnemonic: **DIP FAD**

A.  **D**efamatory and False Statements

    1. A plaintiff does not have to prove that the statement is false, but truth will be an absolute defense.

    2. A statement is defamatory if it tends to detract from a plaintiff's reputation.

    3. A statement is actionable whether it is defamatory on its face or is only defamatory with additional knowledge.

    4. A statement is defamatory even if it was not believed. A plaintiff, however, will have to prove special damages.

    5. A statement must have an element of disgrace in the eyes of at least one respectable segment of society to be considered defamatory. A plaintiff has to show disapproval by a number of relatively respectable people based on the statement.

6. If the statement could have more than one meaning, a judge will determine whether one meaning could possibly be defamatory; if it may a jury will decide if anybody actually interpreted the statement in a defamatory manner.

7. Opinions are not defamatory.

B. Identifying A Plaintiff as the Object of the Statement

1. Groups
A statement that defames a group that is greater than about 25 members is not defamatory.

2. Dead Persons
Negative statements about a dead person are not defamatory.

3. Corporations
Corporations can be defamed, but can only recover for monetary losses.

4. Unnamed Plaintiffs
Statements can be defamatory even if a plaintiff is not directly mentioned by name.

C. Publication
See Ch. 17, III.

D. Fault
A defendant must act either intentionally or negligently; there is no strict liability for defamation. The intent that is required is the intent to publish.

1. Public Figures
A public figure is one who has achieved fame or notoriety, or at least voluntarily enters the public spotlight. Recovery is available only if the defendant acted with malice, i.e., with knowledge that the statements are false or made with reckless disregard as to their truth.

2. Private Persons
Recovery is available if a defendant acted maliciously or negligently.

    a. If a plaintiff does not show malice, the plaintiff has to prove special damages.

    b. If a plaintiff shows malice, damages will be presumed and punitive damages are allowed.

E.    Actual Damages
See Ch. 17, VI.

V.    DEFENSES

A.    Truth
Truth is an absolute defense.

B.    Plaintiff's Consent

C.    Privilege

    1. Absolute Privileges
No liability even if a defendant acted with malice.

        a. Judicial and Legislative Proceedings
All those involved in these proceedings are privileged to make any defamatory remark that is related to the proceedings.

        b. Government Officials
Any official statement made by a government official is privileged. This applies to all federal officials. Courts are split on whether all state officials are protected.

        c. Husband and Wife
Communications between spouses are privileged.

2. Qualified Privileges
The following statements are privileged if they are made without malice:

   a. Reports of a Public Proceeding
   Example: reporting of trials, congressional hearings, etc.

   b. Fair Criticism
   Example: movie reviews and articles of general interest.

   c. Statements Involving the Public Interest
   Example: an article that identifies criminals.

   d. Statements Made for the Interest of the Maker

   e. Statements Made in the Common Interest
   Example: defamatory statements made by a loan company to a bank concerning a prospective loan applicant.

   f. Statements Made For the Interest of the Recipient
   Example: defamatory statements made by a person's former employer to the person's new employer.

## VI. REMEDIES

A. General/Presumed Damages
Damages presumed by law; a plaintiff does not have to prove special damages.

B. Special Damages
A plaintiff who must prove special damages must specifically prove pecuniary loss.

C. Recoverable Damages

   1. Punitive
   In cases of malice only.

2. Damages to Reputation
   These include economic harm.

3. Damages to Feelings
   These include medical bills for a plaintiff's emotional distress.

## CASE CLIPS

**New York Times Co. v. Sullivan (S.Ct. 1964)** Ke, Ep, Fr
**Facts:** Sullivan, a Police Commissioner in Montgomery, Alabama, sued the New York Times for libel after they carried an advertisement that criticized the actions of the Montgomery police. Some of the statements made in the advertisement were erroneous.
**Issue:** May public officials sue for libel?
**Rule:** (Brennan, J.) Public officials cannot recover damages for false defamatory statements unless they can prove that the statements were made with "actual malice" (i.e., with knowledge that they were false or with reckless disregard of whether they were false or not).
**Concurrence:** (Black, J.) Public officials are categorically denied any action of defamation insofar as their public conduct is concerned.

### Old Dominion Branch No. 496, National Association of Letter Carriers v. Austin (S.Ct. 1974) Ke
**Facts:** Austin's name was listed in a union newsletter's "List of Scabs," a list of letter carriers who had failed to pay their union dues.
**Issue:** Are defamatory statements made by a union attempting to organize workers privileged?
**Rule:** (Marshall, J.) Under federal labor law, loose language and undefined slogans are considered part of the give-and-take in economic and political controversies and are privileged statements.

### Janklow v. Newsweek, Inc. (1986) Ke
**Facts:** Newsweek published an article that implied Janklow, a former attorney general, once prosecuted a case out of revenge. Newsweek argued that it was not liable for defamation because the article stated opinion only, not fact.
**Issue:** How does a court determine if a statement is fact or opinion?

**Rule:**  To determine if a statement should be interpreted as fact or opinion, a court must look at four factors: 1) the precision and the specificity of the statement; 2) the verifiability of the statement; 3) the literary context of the statement; and 4) the public context in which the statement was made (i.e., private person v. public figure).

### Philadelphia Newspapers, Inc. v. Hepps (S.Ct. 1986) Ke, Ep

**Facts:**  The defendant published a newspaper article accusing Hepps of using organized crime links to influence governmental processes.

**Issue:**  Which party in a defamation action has the burden of proving the truth of the statements in question?

**Rule:**  (O'Connor, J.)  A plaintiff has the burden of proof to show falsity, as well as fault, before recovering damages for defamation in a matter of public concern. In a matter of private concern, however, a defendant must prove the veracity of the statements.

**Dissent:**  (Stevens, J.)  A plaintiff must only prove fault, not falsity to recover damages for defamation in a matter of public concern.

### Gertz v. Robert Welch, Inc. (S.Ct. 1974) Ke, Ep, Fr

**Facts:**  Gertz was defamed as a "Leninist" by the defendant in a magazine article. The defendants claimed Gertz, a reputable lawyer, was a public figure and thus they had a privilege to criticize him.

**Issue 1:**  When is a person considered a public figure?

**Rule 1:**  (Powell, J.)  When there is clear evidence of general fame or notoriety in a community, or a pervasive involvement in the affairs of society, a person is considered a public figure. A person is not a public figure merely because of an involvement in a matter of public interest.

**Issue 2:**  Can a private figure recover presumed and punitive damages against media defendants for libel in a matter of public concern?

**Rule 2:**  Plaintiffs, in an action for libel involving a matter of public concern, can recover presumed and punitive damages only if they are able to prove actual malice by the media defendants.

**Note:**  Of the four dissenters, two would impose greater restrictions and two would impose lesser restrictions on defamation actions.

### Street v. National Broadcasting Co. (1981) Ke

**Facts:**  NBC produced a television drama of a famous rape trial forty years after it occurred. Street, the rape victim, sued the network for libel for their false portrayal of her. NBC claimed a limited privilege because Street was a public figure.

**Issue:** Does an individual who was once a public figure lose that status with the passage of time?

**Rule:** Once a person becomes a public figure in connection with a particular controversy, that person remains a public figure thereafter for purposes of later commentary or treatment of that controversy. A privilege exists in such cases, requiring a showing of malice before a cause of action for slander will lie.

### Bose Corporation v. Consumers Union of United States, Inc. (S.Ct. 1984) Ke

**Facts:** The Court of Appeals reversed a favorable verdict for Bose. The court held its review of the actual malice determination was not limited to the clearly-erroneous standard of Rule 52(a) of the Federal Rules of Civil Procedure (FRCP).

**Issue:** Does Rule 52(a) of the Federal Rules of Civil Procedure prescribe the standard of review in a determination of actual malice?

**Rule:** (Stevens, J.) The clearly-erroneous standard of Rule 52(a) of the FRCP does not prescribe the standard of review to be applied in reviewing a determination of actual malice. Appellate judges must exercise independent judgment to determine whether the record establishes actual malice with convincing clarity.

### Western Union Tel. Co. v. Lesesne (1952) Ke

**Facts:** Western Union delivered a defamatory telegram to Lesesne.

**Issue:** Is a telegram company liable for defamation on the grounds that delivery of a telegram is publication?

**Rule:** Delivery of a libelous telegram to a person defamed does not constitute publication even if the message reached the hands of a third person, unless the telegraph company expected or should have reasonably expected that the telegram would reach the third person.

### New England Tractor-Trailer Training of Connecticut, Inc v. Globe Newspaper Company (1985) Ke

**Facts:** The Globe published a series of articles that were critical of vocational schools in general and of NETT-MASS specifically. While the plaintiffs, NETT-CONN, were not mentioned specifically in the article, they argued that they were defamed because NETT-MASS and NETT-CONN were part of the same company.

**Issue:** In a defamation action, must a plaintiff prove that the defendant had a subjective intent to defame the plaintiff?

**Rule:** In a defamation suit, a plaintiff must prove that the defendant intended its words to refer to the plaintiff, that the defendant's words could reasonably be interpreted to refer to the plaintiff, and that the defendant was negligent in publishing them in such a way.

### Farnsworth v. Hyde (1973) Ke

**Facts:** Hyde wrote a book about Farnsworth's character, describing Farnsworth as the laziest man in the world.

**Issue:** When is a statement considered defamatory?

**Rule:** Defamation is actionable when statements cause a plaintiff to be subjected to hate or ridicule, and diminish the respect in which the plaintiff is held by a substantial number of people in the community.

### Cinquanta v. Burdett (1963) Ke

**Facts:** The defendant shouted to the plaintiff, his employer, "I don't like doing business with crooks. You're a dead beat." The plaintiff sued for slander and recovered damages for slander per se.

**Issue:** What determines whether a statement is slander per se?

**Rule:** To determine if words are actionable as slander per se, they must be taken in the context and in light of all the circumstances attendant upon the utterances.

### Taylor v. Perkins (1607) Ke

**Facts:** The defendant said to the plaintiff, "Thou art a leprous knave." The plaintiff sued for defamation.

**Issue:** Is a verbal statement that a plaintiff has a disease actionable?

**Rule:** A verbal statement that an individual has a disease is an actionable defamatory utterance.

### Terwilliger v. Wands (1858) Ke, Ep

**Facts:** Terwilliger told a third party that Wands was having sexual relations with a married woman. Wands, upon hearing of Terwilliger's gossip, fell ill and was unable to work.

**Issue:** What type of damages must be shown in a defamation suit based on slander?

**Rule:** A plaintiff must show special damages to recover for slander (i.e., pecuniary damages). Illness and other nonpecuniary damages are insufficient to invoke liability.

### American Broadcasting-Paramount Theatres, Inc. v. Simpson (1962) Ke

**Facts:** The plaintiff, one of two guards who transferred Al Capone between prisons, objected to a TV episode of "The Untouchables" in which a guard is bribed while transferring Capone between prisons.

**Issue 1:** Are TV broadcasts classified as libel or slander?

**Rule 1:** Defamation occurring during a radio or TV broadcast falls under the laws of libel.

**Issue 2:** If it is falsely said that one of two persons has committed a crime, do both have a cause of action for defamation?

**Rule 2:** Any member of a small group which is defamed has a cause of action in libel.

### Bottomley v. F.W. Woolworth & Co., Ltd. (1932) Ke

**Facts:** The defendant, a retail store, sold a magazine which defamed Bottomley without knowing of the magazine's defamatory content.

**Issue:** Is a retailer liable for the sale of defamatory material?

**Rule:** A retailer is not liable for the sale of defamatory material if it did not know of the libel, it had no reason to know of the libel, and it was not negligent in failing to know of the libel.

### Dunlap v. Wayne (1986) Ke

**Facts:** Dunlap sought payments from Wayne for services rendered. Wayne's lawyer wrote to Dunlap's lawyer stating that Wayne refused to pay because the payment was a kick-back. Dunlap saw the letter.

**Issue:** Are statements of opinion on private affairs actionable as defamation?

**Rule:** A defamatory communication may consist of a statement in the form of an opinion, but a statement of this nature is actionable only if it implies the allegation of undisclosed defamatory facts as the basis for the opinion.

## Broadway Approvals Ltd. v. Odhams Press, Ltd. (1965) Ke

**Facts:** The plaintiff used questionable marketing techniques to sell stamps by mail order. Odhams Press wrote a highly critical newspaper article about the plaintiff, intentionally omitting favorable facts.

**Issue:** Is the defense of fair comment defeated if the party acted maliciously?

**Rule:** An honest and fair expression of opinion on a matter of public interest is not actionable even though it is untrue and unjustified unless the publisher acted with malice.

## Dairy Stores, Inc. v. Sentinel Publishing Co., Inc. (1986) Ke

**Facts:** After conducting chemical analyses on the plaintiff's product, Sentinel published articles that the plaintiff's bottled water was not pure spring water, as the plaintiff had advertised.

**Issue:** Does the fair comment privilege apply to statements of fact with respect to matters of legitimate public concern?

**Rule:** The fair comment privilege extends to statements of fact regarding matters of public concern.

## McGranahan v. Dahar (1979) Ke

**Facts:** During a trial, Dahar implied that McGranahan, who was not involved in the trial, had improperly granted a tax abatement to property in which McGranahan held a financial interest.

**Issue:** Are statements made during the course of a trial which are relevant to the trial considered to be defamatory if they are false?

**Rule:** Relevant statements made during a judicial proceeding cannot be defamatory because they are absolutely privileged.

## Chamberlain v. Mathis (1986) Ke

**Facts:** Mathis, the Director of the State Department of Health Services, made several negative statements concerning Chamberlain's job performance.

**Issue:** Does a government official have immunity from liability for defamatory statements made while exercising a discretionary function?

**Rule:** A government official is entitled to qualified immunity for defamatory statements unless the official acted outside his discretionary functions, or with malice.

### Retail Credit Co. v. Russell (1975) Ke

**Facts:** Retail Credit's files on the plaintiff contained incorrect defamatory material which was not changed despite repeated requests.

**Issue:** Is a credit reporting agency privileged to make a libelous statement?

**Rule:** A credit reporting agency has no privilege to make libelous statements.

**Note:** This is the minority rule.

### Mims v. Metropolitan Life Insurance Co. (1952) Ep

**Facts:** Mims, who had worked for Metropolitan Life for 32 years, suspected that he was dismissed because he did not contribute a dollar to a political campaign. Metropolitan Life sent Mims a letter that falsely accused him of inefficiency and unsatisfactory production.

**Issue:** Has a defamatory statement been published if the only persons who heard it were those who wrote the statement and the defamed person?

**Rule:** There has been no publication if the only communication of the defamatory material was among the principal actors themselves and not a third party (i.e., a party other than the one defamed).

**Note:** While the employees who produce the defamatory material on behalf of the corporation are considered to be one entity, if another corporate employee not involved in the activity saw or heard the defamatory material, publication would have occurred.

### Parmiter v. Coupland (1840) Ep

**Facts:** No facts stated.

**Issue:** What constitutes libel?

**Rule:** A publication without justification or lawful excuse which is calculated to injure the reputation of another by exposing that person to hatred, contempt, or ridicule, is libel.

### Youssoupoff v. Metro-Goldwyn-Mayer Pictures (1934) Ep

**Facts:** The plaintiff claimed she was defamed in a fictional movie made by the defendants, which incorrectly portrayed a character closely resembling her as being raped.

**Issue:** When is a defamatory portrayal of a character actionable?

**Rule:** A portrayal of a character is actionable when a jury could reasonably find that a considerable number of reasonable people would identify the character portrayed with the plaintiff and would consider the portrayal defamatory.

### Burton v. Crowell Publishing Co. (1936) Ep

**Facts:** The plaintiff was paid to pose for a picture which was used in the defendant's advertisement. Due to an error, the picture was distorted, making the plaintiff look "grotesque and obscene."
**Issue:** Is a mistaken distortion of one's photograph defamation?
**Rule:** Portraying a person in a manner that subjects the person to ridicule is actionable even if it resulted from a mistake.

### Good Government Group of Seal Beach, Inc. v. Superior Court of Los Angeles County (1978) Ep

**Facts:** The defendant, a local newsletter, published an article criticizing the plaintiff, a city councilman, claiming that he had extorted $100,000 from a land development company in exchange for a building permit.
**Issue:** Is inflammatory rhetoric in the form of an opinion defamation?
**Rule:** Epithets, fiery rhetoric or hyperboles stated as opinion are not actionable.

### E. Hulton & Co. v. Jones (1910) Ep

**Facts:** The defendant published a story about a married man and his mistress. Jones, unbeknownst to the defendant, had a name similar to the man's in the article and people thought the article was about him.
**Issue:** Does lack of intent to injure defeat a defamation action?
**Rule:** Defendants are liable for libel when they defame other people regardless of whether they actually intended to defame those specific people. The main issue is how a statement is understood by others.

### Ellsworth v. Martindale-Hubbell Law Directory, Inc. (1938) Ep

**Facts:** The plaintiff, a lawyer, was listed in the defendant's directory of law firms, but not rated. He had been rated in past editions.
**Issue 1:** Are words considered libelous if their negative connotations are not directly apparent?
**Rule 1:** When words are libel per se (i.e., libel on their face), the courts will presume damages, but when extrinsic facts are needed to establish libel, the words are said to be liable per quod and damages are not awarded unless a plaintiff specifically proves special damages.

**Issue 2:** Is a general loss of customers considered special damages?
**Rule 2:** A general decline of business resulting from the nature of a defendant's words is sufficient to establish special damages.

### Faulk v. Aware, Inc. (1962) Ep

**Facts:** The defendants blacklisted Faulk, a radio and TV performer, as a communist, causing him financial loss. Faulk recovered $4.75 million in damages for libel.
**Issue:** Under what circumstances may a judge overturn a jury damage award in a defamation action?
**Rule:** A judge may overturn a jury's award of compensatory and punitive damages in a defamation action only if the judge rules that the award was not reasonable.

### Faulk v. Aware, Inc. (1963) Ep

**Facts:** Same as above.
**Issue:** How should punitive damages be apportioned between multiple defendants?
**Rule:** Punitive damages should be apportioned between multiple defendants based on their degree of culpability.

### Watt v. Longsden (1930) Ep

**Facts:** Longsden, Watt's supervisor, received a letter from Watt's co-worker that contained false statements about Watt. Longsden showed the letter to the chairman of the company as well as to Watt's wife.
**Issue:** Under what circumstances do privileged defamatory statements become actionable?
**Rule:** Privileged defamatory statements lose their privilege when they exceed the limits of their duty or when they are made with malice.

### Kennedy v. Cannon (1962) Ep

**Facts:** Cannon, the attorney for a man accused of raping Kennedy, was sued for slander after telling a reporter Kennedy had consented.
**Issue:** Does an attorney's immunity from liability for defamation extend to statements made outside the court?
**Rule:** An attorney's privilege against defamation for statements made during a trial does not extend to statements made outside the court.

### Brown & Williamson Tobacco Corp. v. Jacobson (1983) Ep
**Facts:** The defendants broadcasted a damaging story about the plaintiffs based on a summary of a government report. The plaintiffs alleged that the summary was not an accurate reflection of that report.
**Issue:** Under what circumstances might a jury reasonably consider a summary of information unfair?
**Rule:** A rational jury might consider a summary unfair where the libelous effect of the summary exceeds the effect the information would have if read verbatim, i.e., if it has a "greater sting."

### Carr v. Hood (1808) Ep
**Facts:** The defendant wrote a book that was a parody and satire of the plaintiff's book.
**Issue:** Is ridicule of a literary work actionable?
**Rule:** Criticisms of the professional abilities of persons who have placed themselves in the public eye is privileged.

### Curtis Publishing Co. v. Butts
### Associated Press v. Walker (S.Ct. 1967) Ep
**Facts:** These two cases involved the defamation of public figures by the press. In the first case, Butts, a college football coach, was falsely accused of "fixing" a game. In the second case, Walker was alleged to have led a riot against national guardsmen who were escorting black students as part of a racial integration program. Both defendants claimed a privilege because the plaintiffs were public figures.
**Issue:** What is the standard of care that journalists must adhere to when reporting on issues involving public figures?
**Rule:** (Harlan, J.) A public figure who is not a public official can recover damages for a defamatory falsehood on a showing of highly unreasonable conduct constituting an extreme departure from the ordinary standards of investigation and reporting.

### Romaine v. Kallinger (1988) Fr
**Facts:** The defendant published a nonfiction book which stated that Romaine knew "a junkie . . . who was doing time in prison."
**Issue 1:** Is it defamatory as a matter of law to allege that one knows a criminal?
**Rule 1:** While a false attribution of criminality is defamatory as a matter of law, an allegation that one merely knows a criminal is not.

**Issue 2:** When may the question of a statement's defamatory nature be submitted to a jury?

**Rule 2:** The question of a statement's defamatory nature may be submitted to a jury if a court determines that the statement when read by reasonable persons of ordinary intelligence is susceptible to two different meanings, one of which is defamatory.

### Matherson v. Marchello (1984) Fr

**Facts:** The defendants made defamatory statements about Matherson and his wife on a radio talk show.

**Issue:** Is defamation by radio considered to be libel or slander?

**Rule:** Defamation which is broadcasted by means of radio or television is classified as libel.

### Medico v. Time, Inc. (1981) Fr

**Facts:** Time magazine published an article based on an FBI report that linked Medico and his corporation to organized crime.

**Issue:** Is the media privileged to publish defamatory statements that are based on a summary of official government documents?

**Rule:** Publishing a defamatory but accurate and fair synopsis of an official report or proceeding dealing with a subject of public concern is privileged.

**Note:** This is an application of the "fair report privilege."

### Burnett v. National Enquirer, Inc. (1983) Fr

**Facts:** The National Enquirer printed a defamatory article about Carol Burnett which was later retracted. Burnett was awarded both compensatory and punitive damages despite a statutory provision which limited damages for "newspapers" to special damages if a timely retraction was printed.

**Issue:** Do the damage limitations granted in the California retraction statute apply to all newspaper publishers?

**Rule:** The damage limitations granted in the California retraction statute only apply to publishers of newspapers who engage in the immediate dissemination of news such that verification of accuracy is not always possible.

### Waldbaum v. Fairchild Publications, Inc. (1980) Fr
**Facts:** Waldbaum was fired from his position as president of the second largest supermarket in the country. The defendant wrote an article about his ouster and falsely stated that his company had been losing money during the last year. Waldbaum admitted that the defendant acted without malice and the defendant claimed a privilege.
**Issue:** When does an official who is not a public official cease to be a private person and become a public figure?
**Rule:** A person becomes a public figure for limited purposes if the person is attempting to have, or can be expected to have, a major impact on the resolution of a public dispute that has foreseeable and substantial effects on persons beyond its immediate participants.

### Milkovich v. Lorain Journal Co. (S.Ct. 1990) Fr
**Facts:** The defendant published an article which opined and implied that Milkovich had perjured himself.
**Issue:** Are statements of opinion given special constitutional protection under the First Amendment?
**Rule:** (Rehnquist, C.J.) There is no separate constitutional privilege to make defamatory statements of opinion. An opinion is defamatory if a reasonable jury could find that the opinion implied a fact concerning the defendant, and the implied fact can be proven false.
**Dissent:** (Brennan, J.) The rule as stated by the majority is valid, but its application to the facts at hand is incorrect.

### Edwards v. National Audubon Society, Inc. (1977) Fr
**Facts:** Arbib published an article claiming that scientists who argued for the continued use of DDT were "being paid to lie." Arbib told the defendants the names of five scientists, but said he was unsure if they lied. The defendants printed the five names in their newspaper.
**Issue:** If an organization accurately reports a statement against a public figure, even though the organization may have serious doubts of the statement's accuracy, is the report protected under the First Amendment of the Constitution?
**Rule:** When an organization reports serious charges against a public figure, the First Amendment protects the accurate reporting of those charges regardless of the reporter's views regarding their validity.

### Pacella v. Milford Radio Corporation (1984) Fr

**Facts:** Pacella claimed he lost an election because of the defamatory statements that were made by an anonymous caller on the defendant's radio talk show.

**Issue:** Is a broadcaster liable for defamatory statements made about a political candidate during a broadcast?

**Rule:** A broadcaster is prohibited from deleting libelous statements of political candidates and therefore is immune from liability for broadcasting such statements. This reflects the strong public policy in favor of encouraging free and open debate on public issues.

# Chapter 17

## MISUSE OF LEGAL PROCEDURE

I. **MALICIOUS PROSECUTION**

To prevail in a suit for malicious prosecution a plaintiff must prove the following:

Mnemonic: **The Cat Ate My Dog**

A. **T**ermination of the Proceeding in Favor of the Plaintiff
An acquittal, dismissal or dropping of charges are all sufficient. However, a plea bargain does not satisfy this requirement.

B. **C**riminal Proceeding Originally Initiated by the Defendant

1. The defendant must have actively pressed charges and not merely told his story to a law enforcement official who then initiated the proceedings independently.

2. Police and prosecutors are privileged and, therefore, immune from liability for malicious prosecution as long as they generally act within the scope of their duties.

C. **A**bsence of Probable Cause
This exists if the defendant did not actually believe the plaintiff was guilty or if a reasonable person would not have believed that the plaintiff was guilty.

1. Grand Jury Indictments
This will suffice as prima facie evidence of probable cause. However, a failure of the grand jury to indict is not evidence that there was no probable cause.

2. Arrest Warrants
The issuance of an arrest warrant based solely on a police officer's sworn statement is not evidence of probable cause.

3. Reasonable Mistakes
   If a defendant made a reasonable mistake as to the facts or the law, that mistake will excuse a lack of probable cause.

4. Convictions
   A conviction proves probable cause. However, an acquittal will not disprove probable cause because the standard for an acquittal is lower than that for conviction.

D.   Malicious Intent
     The plaintiff must show that the defendant had an improper motive in bringing the proceeding (i.e., not for justice).

E.   Damages
     The plaintiff may recover actual or punitive damages.

II.   WRONGFUL CIVIL PROCEEDINGS

The elements are generally the same as for criminal proceedings. However, it is more difficult to show that the defendant lacked probable cause because the standard for probable cause is lower in civil proceedings than in criminal proceedings.

III.   ABUSE OF PROCESS

Abuse of process is invoked when the criminal or civil action is asserted to bring about a result other than winning the case (e.g., to harass or force settlement). This tort exists when a party has a valid cause of action but sues for wrongful reasons.

## CASE CLIPS

### Russo v. State of New York (1982) Ke

**Facts:** Russo borrowed a car from his brother-in-law. When the car was subsequently stolen, Russo impersonated his brother-in-law and reported the theft to the insurance company and the police. A police officer discovered the plaintiff's impersonation and arrested him. The charges were dismissed and Russo sued for malicious prosecution.

**Issue 1:** What must a plaintiff prove in an action for malicious prosecution?

**Rule 1:** A plaintiff can recover for malicious prosecution by establishing that (1) the defendant commenced or continued a criminal proceeding against the plaintiff, (2) the proceeding terminated in the plaintiff's favor, (3) there was no probable cause for the proceeding, and (4) the proceeding was instituted in actual malice.

**Issue 2:** Does the issuance of an arrest warrant by a judge raise a presumption of probable cause which would defeat a malicious prosecution claim?

**Rule 2:** An arrest warrant is not evidence of probable cause when the warrant was issued because of the defendant's sworn statement, as opposed to an arrest warrant issued after a grand jury indictment.

### Friedman v. Dozorc (1981) Ke

**Facts:** Dozorc, an attorney, sued Dr. Friedman on behalf of one of Friedman's patients who had died. When the case was dismissed, Friedman sued Dozorc for bringing a frivolous action.

**Issue:** Does an attorney owe a duty of care to an adverse party to avoid bringing frivolous claims?

**Rule:** An attorney does not owe a duty to an adverse party to avoid frivolous suits.

### Bull v. McCluskey (1980) Ke

**Facts:** Bull, an attorney, brought a malpractice suit against McCluskey, a doctor, on behalf of one of McCluskey's patients to coerce a money settlement. Bull knew there were no grounds for the suit and did not introduce any expert testimony at trial. Bull claimed that he did not act out of malice.

**Issue:** Is malice an element of an action for abuse of process?

**Rule:** Malice is not required for abuse of process. Abuse of process involves any suit asserted for a motive other than winning.

### Gregoire v. Biddle (1949) Ke

**Facts:** The plaintiff, a Frenchman, was arrested upon entering the United States for being German. He was detained from 1942 to 1946 despite a ruling by the Enemy Alien Hearing Board that he was

French. The plaintiff sued various government officials responsible for his illegal detention for malicious prosecution.

**Issue:** Is a United States Attorney immune from civil liability for malicious prosecution?

**Rule:** Department of Justice employees are absolutely immune from civil liability for malicious prosecution.

## Melvin v. Pence (1942) Ke

**Facts:** Pence, a detective hired to follow Melvin, a married man, confronted Melvin when he was with another woman. Melvin instituted proceedings before the state licensing authorities to revoke Pence's license, but Pence won. Pence sued for malicious prosecution.

**Issue:** Can an action for malicious prosecution arise from an administrative action?

**Rule:** A suit for malicious prosecution may be brought for the wrongful institution of administrative proceedings, in addition to the wrongful institution of judicial proceedings.

# Chapter 18

## PRIVACY

## I. PRIVATE FACTS

A party is liable for publicly disclosing embarrassing private facts about a plaintiff.

A. Embarrassing
The published facts must be very embarrassing to a reasonable person. An extra-sensitive plaintiff will not recover.

B. Of No Public Concern
The published facts cannot be of legitimate public concern or they will be privileged under *Time v. Hill.*

Note: A privilege to disclose private facts may extend to private persons who were formerly in the public eye.

C. Publicized
The information must be publicized to more than a few people.

D. Not of Public Knowledge
The information cannot be a matter of public knowledge.

## II. APPROPRIATION

Involves the use of the plaintiff's name or likeness for the commercial advantage of the defendant without receiving the plaintiff's permission or agreement.

A. Invasion
There is no requirement that the defendant invade a private area of the plaintiff's life; it is enough to use the name or likeness without permission.

B.  Commercial Advertisements
Usually it is limited to commercial advertisements, e.g., if a newspaper uses a picture of a woman next to an article about women as an illustration, no appropriation has been made.

## III.  INTRUSION UPON SECLUSION

Protects a person's rights to seclusion and solitude in all private affairs. This interest is usually balanced against the First Amendment free speech interest.

A.  Reasonable Person
The intrusion must be objectionable to a reasonable person, not just the particular plaintiff.

B.  Personal Gain
A defendant is liable even if there was no personal gain.

C.  Private Place
The intrusion must be into a private place of the plaintiff.

D.  Electronic Surveillance
Always considered an unreasonable invasion of a private place. Journalists never have a First Amendment privilege to use electronic surveillance devices.

E.  Intent
The defendant's purpose must be to harm the plaintiff's interests.

## IV.  FALSE LIGHT

Involves placing a person before the public in a false light, i.e., painting an image of the plaintiff that would be objectionable to a reasonable person.

A.  False Light Occurs When:

1. One is said to have views one does not in fact have; or

2. One is said to have done something one did not in fact do.

B. Intent
If the published information involves the public interest, a plaintiff must prove that the defendant acted with malicious intent. See Ch. 16.

C. Reasonably Sensitive
An extra-sensitive plaintiff may not recover.

V. DEFENSES

A. Consent
A plaintiff who consents to an invasion of privacy cannot sue. A gratuitous consent may be revoked anytime before the actual invasion occurs.

B. Defamation Defenses
The privileges that exist in defamation are also privileges for the invasion of privacy. See Ch. 16, V, C.

Exceptions: Truth and absence of malice are not valid defenses to the invasion of privacy. However, the absence of malice may be a defense if the facts are newsworthy.

VI. DAMAGES

A. Special damages need not be proven.

B. This is a personal right and the action will not survive if the plaintiff dies before the suit is resolved.

C. Corporations cannot recover for the invasion of privacy.

# CASE CLIPS

## Cantrell v. Forest City Publishing Co. (S.Ct. 1974) Ke, Fr

**Facts:** Cantrell, the wife of a man killed by a bridge collapse, sued the defendant newspaper for an article it published which contained numerous false and inaccurate statements about the family.

**Issue:** May publishers be vicariously liable for the actions of their employees on a "false light" theory of invasion of privacy?

**Rule:** (Stewart, J.) Publishers may be liable for invasion of privacy under the doctrine of respondeat superior for articles written by employees acting within the scope of their employment.

## Hustler Magazine v. Falwell (S.Ct. 1988) Ke, Ep

**Facts:** Falwell, a well known minister, was the subject of a parody in Hustler Magazine that falsely described his first sexual encounter.

**Issue:** Must a public figure prove "actual malice" to recover for intentional infliction of emotional distress?

**Rule:** (Rehnquist, C.J.) To recover for the intentional infliction of emotional distress a public figure must prove actual malice.

## Nelson v. Times (1977) Ke

**Facts:** Nelson sued for invasion of privacy and emotional distress after the defendant published an unauthorized picture of her son in connection with a book review in their newspaper.

**Issue:** Does the publication of a person's photograph in a publication constitute an invasion of privacy?

**Rule:** Unauthorized use of a person's photograph in a publication is not an invasion of privacy if it is not an unreasonable intrusion upon the seclusion of a person, an appropriation of a person's name or likeness for financial benefit, unreasonable publicity of a person's private life, or publicity that places a person in a false light.

**Note:** Invasion of privacy is a personal tort that can only be asserted by the person harmed.

## Vogel v. W. T. Grant Co. (1974) Ke

**Facts:** The defendant informed third parties of the plaintiff's debts in order to coerce him to pay.

**Issue:** Is the publicizing of a person's debts to a selected and limited group of people an invasion of privacy?

**Rule:** Notification of a small number of third parties that a plaintiff did not pay off debts is not sufficient to constitute the publication component of the invasion of privacy tort. However, notification of the general public would be unreasonable and actionable.

### O'Neil v. Schuckardt (1986) Ke

**Facts:** The defendants convinced O'Neil's wife to divorce him since he was not a member of their church. They also told O'Neil's children that O'Neil was not their true father. O'Neil sued for alienation of affections and invasion of privacy.

**Issue:** Is the cause of action for alienation of affections still viable?

**Rule:** The cause of action for alienation of affections is abolished.

### Dietemann v. Time, Inc. (1971) Ke, Fr

**Facts:** Life Magazine's employees entered Dietemann's home under false pretenses and used hidden cameras and tape recorders to collect data for a story that was later published.

**Issue:** Does the First Amendment give journalists an immunity from liability for torts committed while gathering news?

**Rule:** The First Amendment has never been construed to accord reporters immunity from crimes or torts such as invasion of privacy committed in the course of news gathering.

### Roberson v. Rochester Folding Box Co. (1902) Ep

**Facts:** The defendant used Roberson's picture in its advertising campaign without Roberson's permission.

**Issue:** Can one who has not been defamed assert an action for the unauthorized use of one's likeness?

**Rule:** Damages and an injunction are not granted for invasion of privacy by the unauthorized use of one's likeness because allowing such suits would result in a vast amount of litigation.

**Note:** This decision was quickly overruled.

### Sidis v. F-R Publishing Corp. (1940) Ep

**Facts:** The defendants published an article about Sidis, a former child prodigy who had been out of the public eye for over fifteen years.

**Issue:** Is it an invasion of privacy to report a public occurrence or the contents of a public record after a significant amount of time has lapsed?

**Rule:** Publishing the happening of a public occurrence or the contents of a public record is not actionable, as long as it is still a matter of public interest, no matter how much time has lapsed.

### Tropeano v. Atlantic Monthly Co. (1980) Ep

**Facts:** Tropeano's picture appeared alongside an article in the defendant's magazine. No other reference to the plaintiff was made.
**Issue:** Are plaintiffs entitled to compensation if their photographs are published without their permission?
**Rule:** Plaintiffs can recover for the unauthorized use of their photographs only if the use was deliberate and for commercial gain.

### Zacchini v. Scripps-Howard Broadcasting Co. (S.Ct. 1977) Ep, Fr

**Facts:** The defendants videotaped Zacchini's "human cannonball" act and broadcast it on a local television station without his consent.
**Issue:** Does the media's privilege to report newsworthy matters extend to a broadcast of an entire performance without the consent of the participant?
**Rule:** (White, J.) The media privilege to report a newsworthy performance does not extend to filming and broadcasting an entire act when the participant does not consent to the broadcast.

### Factors Etc., Inc. v. Pro Arts, Inc. (1978) Ep

**Facts:** The plaintiff owned an exclusive license to commercially exploit the likeness of Elvis Presley. The defendant independently marketed a memorial poster shortly after the singer's death.
**Issue:** Does an exclusive right of publicity transferred during a person's lifetime still remain exclusive after the person dies?
**Rule:** The right of publicity may be validly transferred during the owner's life to one who may prevent a third party from using the publicity for commercial gain, even after the subject's death.

### Briscoe v. Reader's Digest (1971) Ep

**Facts:** Reader's Digest published an article mentioning Briscoe by name and describing a hijacking he had committed 11 years earlier.
**Issue:** Are reports of past crimes protected by the First Amendment?
**Rule:** Truthful reports of crimes and those involved are newsworthy and are therefore protected by the First Amendment. However, a

report about a reformed criminal who has avoided publicity for a long time serves little public purpose, and is an invasion of privacy.

### Cox Broadcasting Corp. v. Cohn (S.Ct. 1975) Ep
**Facts:** A television station violated state laws by revealing the name of a deceased rape victim. The reporter learned the name by looking at the indictments against the rapist, which were on public record.
**Issue:** Is the publication of public information prohibited by state law actionable on the grounds of invasion of privacy?
**Rule:** (White, J.) Invasion of privacy cannot be raised for published information already part of the public record because it is protected by the Constitution.

### Time, Inc. v. Hill (S.Ct. 1967) Ep
**Facts:** Time published an article stating that a Broadway play was actually a re-enactment of Hill's ordeal when he was held as a hostage several years earlier. Hill sued for portraying him in a "false light."
**Issue:** Is a publication that erroneously portrays a person in a "false light" liable for invasion of privacy?
**Rule:** (Brennan, J.) A person is liable for invasion of privacy in "false light" cases only if a plaintiff can prove that the person knew of the falsity or acted with reckless disregard of it.

### Nader v. General Motors (1970) Ep, Fr
**Facts:** General Motors attempted to discourage Nader, a well-known consumer activist, from publishing a book criticizing their automobiles.
**Issue:** Has a person committed an invasion of privacy if the person interviewed a party's acquaintances about the party's personal life, followed the party in public, attempted to entrap the party, made harassing phone calls to the party, tapped the party's phone, or conducted a harassing investigation?
**Rule:** Wiretapping and eavesdropping comprise a prima facie case of invasion of privacy. Interviewing friends, harassing phone calls, and attempted entrapment are not invasions of privacy. Surveillance is actionable only if the defendant was excessively obtrusive.

### Galella v. Onassis (1973) Ep, Fr
**Facts:** Galella, a photographer known for harassing celebrities, was detained because of his attempts to secure information about Onassis.

**Issue:** May the public's right to know impinge on a public figure's right to privacy?

**Rule:** Legitimate countervailing social needs warrant some intrusions despite an individual's reasonable expectation of privacy and freedom from harassment.

### Gilbert v. Medical Economics Co. (1981) Fr

**Facts:** The magazine Medical Economics published an article about two cases of alleged malpractice by the plaintiff. The plaintiff sued for defamation because the article suggested that her malpractice was related to her history of psychiatric and personal problems, and included her name and photograph.

**Issue:** Does the First Amendment give the press the right to disclose private embarrassing facts about individuals who are not public officials or public figures?

**Rule:** The press may disclose private embarrassing facts about a private individual if the facts are independently newsworthy or have a substantial nexus (i.e., connection) with a newsworthy topic.

### The Florida Star v. B.J.F. (S.Ct. 1989) Fr

**Facts:** The Florida Star newspaper violated a state statute that made it unlawful to publish the name of a victim of a sexual offense. The newspaper obtained the plaintiff's name from a police report.

**Issue:** Is a state statute that prohibits the publication of truthful information a violation of the First Amendment?

**Rule:** (Marshall, J.) Publication of truthful information which is lawfully obtained may be prohibited by a state statute only when the statute protects a state interest of the highest order.

**Concurrence:** (Scalia, J.) A law cannot be regarded as protecting an interest of the highest order when the law leaves appreciable damage to that supposedly vital interest unprohibited.

### Carson v. Here's Johnny Portable Toilets, Inc. (1983) Fr

**Facts:** Carson, a well-known entertainer, sued the defendants for invasion of the rights of privacy and publicity after they marketed a line of toilets named "Here's Johnny Portable Toilets." The phrase "Here's Johnny" was commonly associated with Carson.

**Issue:** Is a celebrity's right of publicity invaded if neither the celebrity's name nor likeness is used?

**Rule:** A celebrity's right of publicity is invaded whenever the celebrity's identity is intentionally appropriated for commercial purposes. Identity is not limited to the celebrity's name or likeness; it includes any characteristic that is clearly associated with the celebrity.
**Note:** The right of publicity protects against commercial exploitation of a celebrity's identity, whereas the right of privacy protects a person's right "to be let alone."

# Chapter 19

## INTERFERENCE WITH ADVANTAGEOUS RELATIONSHIPS

I.    INJURIOUS FALSEHOOD

A.    Trade Libel
Trade libel is a cause of action against a party who has made false statements concerning a plaintiff's business or product. The plaintiff must prove the following elements:

Mnemonic: **SIPS**

    1. False Statement
    The party made a false statement about the plaintiff's property, business or product,

    2. Intent
    The party:

        a. Acted with reckless disregard as to the statement's truth,

        b. Knew the statement was false, or

        c. Acted with malice.

    3. Publication
    The statement was communicated to and understood by a third party, and

    4. Special Damages
    The plaintiff suffered special damages due to the statement (i.e., pecuniary loss).

B.    Slander of Title
Slander of title is an action against a party who has made false statements about a plaintiff's right to property. The elements are the same as for trade libel, except this tort involves property.

For example, Susan falsely claims that she owns Rob's land and causes him damage because a potential buyer of the land backs out of the deal.

C.  Defenses to Injurious Falsehood

    1. Truth
    Truth is an absolute defense.

    2. Privilege
    A party may raise any privilege that could be raised in a defamation case. See Ch.16, V, C.

    3. Competition by Fair Means
    A party is allowed to make generally truthful comparisons between its product and a plaintiff's product.

    4. Rival Claimant's Privilege
    A party is allowed to challenge a plaintiff's ownership of property if a reasonable person would think that the party may have a possessory interest in the property, even if the party does not actually have one.

II.  INTERFERENCE WITH AN EXISTING CONTRACT

This is an action against a third party who induces a party to breach a contract.

A.  Elements

    1. The plaintiff must be a party to the contract.

    2. The third party must induce a party to the contract to breach its contractual obligations to the plaintiff.

    3. Intent
    It must be shown that the third party:

      a. Knew about the contract's existence,

b. Knew its actions would lead to a breach of the contract, and

c. Actively interfered with the contract. Merely offering a better price or a better deal is not enough.

4. Damages
The plaintiff can recover for profits lost, any emotional harm suffered, and for punitive damages. The plaintiff, however, cannot recover twice (i.e., from both the breaching party and the inducer).

B. Defenses

1. This tort does not apply to the following contracts:

a. Illegal contracts,

b. Marriage contracts,

c. Contracts terminable at will, and

d. Unenforceable contracts.

Note: All illegal contracts are unenforceable contracts, but not all unenforceable contracts are illegal contracts.

2. Privileges
A party is privileged to interfere with an existing contractual relationship in the following instances:

a. Protection of One's Own Position
A party not trying to develop new business may make statements to protect its existing contract rights.

b. Social Interests
A party may induce a breach if the breach promotes social welfare.

## III.  INTERFERENCE WITH A PROSPECTIVE ADVANTAGE

This is an action against a party who causes a plaintiff to lose possible future contracts. The elements are basically the same as for interference with an existing contract, except that the party has a greater privilege to interfere.

A.  Privilege
A party is privileged to interfere with a prospective contractual relationship when:

1. The party is acting to pursue its own business interests.

2. The party is not merely trying to bankrupt the plaintiff.

3. The party is not acting out of pure malice; mixed emotions are allowed if there is a legitimate business interest involved.

4. The party honestly advises somebody not to deal with the plaintiff (e.g., advice given by a friend or a relative).

B.  Interference with a plaintiff's benefit from prospective non-business related matters can also be actionable (e.g., if Susan induced Rob's father to leave Rob out of his will, Susan might be liable for tortious interference).

## IV.  INTERFERENCE WITH FAMILY RELATIONS

This is an action against a party that causes one to lose the affections of a family member.

A.  Husband and Wife
A plaintiff who sues a defendant for seducing its spouse must prove:

1. The defendant willfully or maliciously seduced the spouse.

2. At the outset, the spouse did not voluntarily accept the seduction.

3. The spouse did not actively contribute to the seduction.

4. The plaintiff was not at fault for causing the spouse to stray.

5. The loss of affection was caused by the defendant's actions.

B.   Alienation of a Child's Affections
No cause of action exists against a party that causes a parent to lose a child's affection unless the party:

1. induces the child to leave home. However, causing a child to leave home for marriage purposes is a privileged action.

2. has sexual intercourse with a female child who is a minor.

C.   Alienation of a Parent's Affections
There is no recovery available to a child against a third party who causes the child to lose the affection of a parent.


## CASE CLIPS

**National Association for the Advancement of Colored People v. Claiborne Hardware Company (S.Ct. 1982) Ke**
**Facts:** The NAACP organized a boycott of the white merchants of Claiborne County. The boycott was effectuated by the peaceful exercise of First Amendment rights as well as some individual acts of violence. Based on the tort of malicious interference, the merchants were awarded damages for all their business losses.
**Issue:** Will the exercise of First Amendment rights support an award of damages for malicious interference?
**Rule:** (Stevens, J.) While a state may legitimately impose damages for the consequences of violent conduct, it may not award compensation for the consequences of nonviolent, protected activities. Only those losses proximately caused by unlawful conduct may be recovered in an action for malicious interference.

### Abrahams v. Kidney (1870) Ke
**Facts:**  The defendant seduced the plaintiff's minor daughter. The daughter became ill afterwards and was unable to work for the plaintiff.

**Issue:**  Is compensation for interference with family relations due to seduction limited to losses caused by pregnancy or venereal disease?

**Rule:**  Damages are not limited to those resulting from pregnancy or venereal disease in cases involving interference with family relations arising from a seduction.

### Borer v. American Airlines, Inc. (1977) Ke
**Facts:**  The plaintiffs, children of a woman who was injured by the defendant's negligence, sued the defendant for the loss of parental consortium.

**Issue:**  Can children sue to recover damages for the loss of the services, companionship, affection and guidance of a parent?

**Rule:**  There is no common law recovery by a child for the loss of parental consortium.

**Note:**  The courts will allow a spouse to sue for loss of consortium.

### Lumley v. Gye (1853) Ep
**Facts:**  The plaintiff held an exclusive contract for the performance of an opera singer. The defendant, knowing of the plaintiff's contract, maliciously induced the singer to breach the contract.

**Issue:**  Does a party whose contract has been breached because of the malicious intrusions of a third party have a cause of action against the third party?

**Rule:**  One who maliciously induces another to breach a contract is liable for the interference.

### Tarleton v. M'Gawley (1793) Ep
**Facts:**  The plaintiff engaged in trade with natives along the coast of Africa. The defendant, claiming that the natives owed him money, shot at them and thus scared them from trading with the plaintiff.

**Issue:**  Is a party liable for improper conduct that results in the loss of another's prospective business?

**Rule:**  One is liable for the intentional interference with another's prospective economic advantage.

### People Express Airlines, Inc. v.
### Consolidated Rail Corp. (1985) Ep, Fr

**Facts:** People Express was forced to evacuate its terminal located within one mile of Consolidated Rail Corp.'s freight yard, after a dangerous chemical escaped from one of the defendant's railway tank cars.

**Issue:** Is a defendant who negligently interferes with a plaintiff's business, causing pure economic losses unaccompanied by property damage or personal injury, liable in tort?

**Rule:** A negligent party is liable to foreseeable plaintiffs for economic losses proximately caused by its breach of duty to avoid the risk of economic injury.

### Mogul Steamship Co. v. McGregor, Gow, & Co. (1889) Ep

**Facts:** The defendants formed a shipping association, offering a five percent rebate to those who dealt exclusively with their group. The plaintiff, a rival shipper, claimed that the defendants were trying to run him out of business.

**Issue:** Can an action for unfair competition be asserted without proof of ill-will or illegality?

**Rule:** Competitive actions are not actionable unless they are dishonest, intimidating, or illegal.

### International News Service v. Associated Press (S.Ct. 1918) Ep

**Facts:** The I.N.S. and the A.P. were both in the business of gathering and distributing news. The I.N.S. started taking the news gathered and published by the A.P. in one part of the country and publishing it in other parts before the A.P. could publish it there.

**Issue:** Is it an unfair trade practice for one to distribute information gathered by another party at great expense for one's own profit?

**Rule:** (Pitney, J.) Information is quasi-property to those who gather and distribute it at an expense for commercial gain. Exploiting another's property before the owner is able to use it is an unfair trade practice.

**Dissent:** (Brandeis, J.) Knowledge, truth, conceptions and ideas are free for common use after they have been voluntarily communicated, with the limited exception of material which is protected under patent and copyright law.

### Ely-Norris Safe Co. v. Mosler Safe Co. (1925)
### Mosler Safe Co. v. Ely Norris Safe Co. (S.Ct. 1926) Ep

**Facts:** The defendant sold safes which were similar in appearance to the plaintiff's brand safe, but which were of inferior quality. The similarity caused confusion between the two brands, prompting the plaintiff to sue for unfair competition.

**Issue:** Can a party recover damages from a competitor who uses deceit to gain customers?

**Rule:** (Holmes, J.) A party may recover damages for the deceptive actions of a competitor if it can prove actual lost sales.

### Credit Alliance Corporation v.
### Arthur Andersen & Co. (1985) Fr

**Facts:** Credit Alliance Corporation relied on an erroneous financial analysis of a private company prepared by Arthur Andersen & Co.

**Issue:** Absent privity of contract, is an accountant liable to a party that relies to its detriment upon a negligently prepared report?

**Rules:** An accountant is liable to a third party for a negligently prepared report if it was known the reports were to be used for a particular purpose.

### Imperial Ice Co. v. Rossier (1941) Fr

**Facts:** Imperial Ice bought an ice distributing company with an agreement that the former owner would not compete with Imperial Ice. The defendants, another ice distributing company, induced the former owner to breach this clause.

**Issue:** Is one who induces a third party to breach a contract liable when the inducement is for economic gain?

**Rule:** One seeking to advance one's own economic interests is not privileged to induce a third party to breach a contract.

### Katz v. Kapper (1935) Fr

**Facts:** Kapper forced Katz out of business by selling his goods at a loss and threatening Katz's customers.

**Issue:** What methods of competition are lawful?

**Rule:** A threat is unlawful only if it is a threat to do an unlawful act. Competition in business is not actionable, even if it ruins a rival, as long as the methods do not involve wrongful conduct.

**Note:**   When defendants have a legitimate commercial interest a court will generally ignore the presence of malicious motivations.

## TABLE OF CASES

# SULZBURGER & GRAHAM PUBLISHING
### 505 Eighth Avenue
### New York, NY 10018

## 800-366-7086

## ORDER FORM

Name: _____     Phone: _____

Shipping address: _____     Law School: _____
(No PO Boxes)
_____     Graduation: _____

City/State/Zip: _____

Credit Card #: _____     Expiration: _____

Signature: _____

### BLOND'S LAW GUIDES $15.99

___ Torts
___ Torts, Prosser Ed.
___ Torts, Henderson Ed.
___ Property
___ Property, Dukeminier Ed.
___ Evidence
___ Contracts
___ Contracts, Farnsworth Ed.
___ Family Law
___ Income Tax
___ Corporations
___ Criminal Law
___ Civil Procedure
___ Civil Procedure, Yeazell Ed.

___ International Law
___ Constitutional Law
___ Administrative Law
___ Commercial Law
___ Criminal Procedure

### BLOND'S ESSAY SERIES $21.99
___ Torts
___ Contracts

### BLOND'S MULTIPLE CHOICE $29.99
___ Multistate Questions

### BAR EXAM ESSAY $24.99
___ Scoring High On Bar Exam Essays

### Shipping Information
)UPS Ground: $3.00 per order
)
)Second Day Air (3 day if ordered late):
)$7.00 first book, $1.00 each additional book

)Next Day Air:
)$10.00 first two books, $3.00 each
)additional book
)Saturday delivery an additional $10.00

Delivery time will vary, based on distance from New York City. Washington/Boston corridor can expect delivery 2 working days after shipment. West Coast should allow 6 working days, unless Second Day or Next Day Air is specified when ordering.

**PLEASE MAKE CHECKS AND MONEY ORDERS PAYABLE TO:     SULZBURGER & GRAHAM PUBLISHING**